HERB AND HONEY COOKERY

An exciting collection of original recipes using these versatile, natural ingredients to accentuate the flavors of delicious whole food dishes

By the same author
FAST VEGETARIAN FEASTS
GARLIC COOKERY
THE VEGETARIAN FEAST

HERB AND HONEY COOKERY

by
MARTHA ROSE SHULMAN

Illustrated by Rita Greer

THORSONS PUBLISHERS INC.
New York

Thorsons Publishers Inc.
377 Park Avenue South
New York, New York 10016

First U.S. Edition 1985

© MARTHA ROSE SHULMAN 1985

All rights reserved. No part of this book may be reproduced or utilized in any form or by any means, electronic or mechanical, including photocopying and recording, or by any information storage and retrieval system, without permission in writing from the publisher. Inquiries should be addressed to Thorsons Publishers Inc.

LIBRARY OF CONGRESS CATALOGING IN PUBLICATION DATA

Shulman, Martha Rose.
  Herb and honey cookery.

  Includes index.
  1. Cookery (Herbs) 2. Cookery (Honey) I. Title.
TX819.H4S58   1985   641.6'57   84-24033
ISBN 0-7225-1050-0

Printed and bound in Great Britain

Thorsons Publishers Inc. are distributed to the trade by Inner Traditions International Ltd., New York

CONTENTS

		Page
	Introduction	7
I.	Breakfasts	25
II.	Breads	40
III.	Soups	61
IV.	Vegetables, Legumes, Grains, Tofu, and Pasta	78
V.	Dairy Products and Eggs	106
VI.	Salads	123
VII.	Sauces, Dressings, and Condiments	143
VIII.	Desserts	162
	Index of Herb Recipes	187
	Index of Honey Recipes	189
	General Index	191

INTRODUCTION

Why herbs and honey in the same book? Because both honey and herbs have been used for thousands of years to season foods of all kinds. Sugar and salt are relatively recent condiments, and ones we should learn to do if not without, with much less, as our society's blood pressure begins to rise, its girths begin to widen, and heart disease and diabetes become increasingly more widespread. What is sad about our over-use of salt and sugar, aside from what it is doing to our health, is that we have practically forgotten about the joys of fresh herbs and the various honeys.

This book is not a low-sodium cookbook, although salt can certainly be omitted from the recipes, but a collection of recipes whose purpose is to expose you to all the herbs I adore, and to honey cookery. Discovering herbs is like discovering *food*. You will find flavors you never imagined, and you will make dishes that evoke inevitable exclamations of "*What* is this marvelous *taste*?"

HERBS

I have never had a real vegetable garden, but I have always grown herbs. When I lived in Texas, every year I would buy seedlings, and plant them in big plastic buckets I gathered from fast-food restaurants (I think their pickles came in them). My herb garden was a strange looking collection of these pots, which lined my driveway, the sunniest area at my house. My basil, fennel, dill, parsley, and marjoram grew to monumental heights, and I had bushy pots of thyme, mint, rosemary, and sage. What a joy it was to come up my driveway every afternoon; I would immediately begin thinking about dinner. Just a few leaves of marjoram or thyme in a salad, basil in a soup or tomato sauce, *fines herbes* in an omelette, made me feel like I was living a luxurious life.

In Paris my herb garden is much more modest, a few pots on my balcony. But it provides me with the same magic, and I am always running out for a few sprigs of thyme or rosemary, parsley or chives, basil or chervil, to add to a dish and transport me to the Mediterranean. For herbs infuse a dish with sunshine; they are springtime on the palate. Probably more than any other food, herbs, with their distinctive flavors, have a kind of Proustian power. If you discovered fresh coriander in a family restaurant in Mexico, then coriander will always mean Mexico to you, even when you find it in a Chinese or Indian dish. Rosemary, thyme, and basil bring me right back to the kitchen of the Provençal farmhouse I have summered in twice. Marjoram brings me to my little house in Austin, Texas, because the plant I had there was such a thriving one, and I included the herb in so many of the meals I cooked.

This is not to say that you have to have an herb garden, or live in Provence or Texas, to appreciate and benefit from fresh herbs. Greengrocers, markets, and even supermarkets are beginning to sell more than the ubiquitous parsley; a demand can be created if enough people begin to ask for fresh herbs. Jump at the opportunity whenever you see fresh basil, tarragon, chervil, or thyme; take some home and keep it in a plastic container in your refrigerator (see instructions for storing herbs, page 9), and use the herbs in the recipes that follow, or experiment on your own. Take advantage of friends who do grow them; they will always have extra to spare.

As with all things gastronomic, personal taste will come into play in a big way here. You may find that you just don't like sage, or coriander, or caraway seeds (but I've never met a person who didn't love basil). You will find that a very small quantity of certain herbs added to a dish will suffice, whereas other dishes call for more, and some, like pesto, depend on large quantities of a particular herb. Elizabeth David, in her introduction to *Summer Cooking* (Penguin, 1955, 1965), couldn't be more eloquent and correct when she says:

> The quantity in which any given herb is to be used is a matter of taste rather than of rule. Cookery books are full of exhortations to discretion in this matter, but much depends on the herb with which you happen to be dealing, what food it is to flavour, whether the dish in question is to be a long simmered one in which it is the sauce which will be ultimately flavoured with the herbs, or whether the herbs are to go into a stuffing . . . in which case the aromas will be more concentrated, or again whether the herbs will be cooked only a minute or two . . . or not cooked at all . . . whether the herbs are dried or fresh.

She then goes on to call attention to dishes in which fresh herbs are the essential flavoring, like pesto, and states that:

> Sometimes it is a good thing to forget that basil, parsley, mint, tarragon, fennel, are all bunched together under the collective word 'herbs' and to remember that the difference between leaf vegetables (sorrel, spinach, lettuce) is very small, and indeed at one time all these plants were known collectively as 'salad herbs'. Nobody

tells you to 'use spinach with caution', and neither can you be 'discreet with basil' when you are making a pesto sauce, because basil is the essential flavouring . . .

Herb Gardens

The most important thing to remember, whether growing herbs in a garden or in pots, is that they like well-drained soil, and with the exception of the mints, full sunlight. Just imagine the conditions on the Mediterranean hillsides where many of them normally grow wild. They don't require great soil and they aren't finicky. Most can be started from seed (tarragon is the exception), or you can buy small plants at nurseries. For home cooking, small pots of herbs are usually sufficient, unless you want to make large quantities of pesto, and you can keep these in a sunny window or on a patio. A handsome garden consisting of one- to two-foot plots for each herb you wish to grow will provide you with more than enough for spring, summer, and autumn. You can dry what is left over for the winter.

Storing Fresh Herbs

Opinions differ on how best to store fresh herbs. Until I read Elizabeth David I thought the only way was to put bunches of fresh herbs in a jar of water and cover tightly with a plastic bag, securing the bag to the jar with a rubber band; or to wet several thicknesses of paper towel, line the bottom of a jar, and store the herbs in the jar, tightly sealed. Both these methods work well if you are keeping the herbs for up to four or five days. But if you want to keep them longer they should be kept, absolutely dry, in a tightly sealed plastic container, a jar, or plastic bag. The important thing is to keep them dry. Some herbs, like basil, will turn black very quickly, and it is best to blend basil up into a pesto at once, if that is what you are planning for it, omitting the garlic and cheese until you are ready to serve, or to cover the leaves with olive oil. Other herbs, like tarragon and chervil, can be worked into a herb butter and kept for several days. But I have successfully kept both these herbs in the refrigerator, well-wrapped and dry, for several days. In Provence I bought basil in little pots, which I kept in a bowl of water so they wouldn't dry out. If I hadn't used up the basil so quickly they would have lasted for weeks like this.

Drying Herbs

If you have more herbs than you can use, and winter is coming on, the only thing to do is to dry them. The resulting herbs will get you through the winter and will be much more fragrant than commercially dried ones.

Certain herbs dry better than others. Those that do *not* dry well are parsley, chives, and the leaves of fennel. Dill seems to lose most of its flavor when dried. Because of the loss of their volatile oils, rosemary, sage, and marjoram are less strong in their dried state. All herbs except mint take on a certain mustiness or bitterness when dried, and they cannot be employed in the same way as fresh ones. Always reduce the quantity of a fresh herb by a half to two-thirds if substituting the dried version. Their flavors are sometimes completely different; what they lack, often, is the sweetness of fresh herbs. But sometimes it is exactly that savory, earthy flavor you want. This is certainly true of dried thyme, when I use it in bean pâtés and soups and stews, of sage when I use it in breads, of oregano in Italian food. Basil, however, is an herb that loses its most memorable qualities in drying. It is still a powerful and good seasoning, especially in soups and slowly simmered sauces and vegetable dishes, but you could never make a pesto with it.

Harvest herbs for drying on a dry day, when they are just beginning to flower. Lay them on newspapers, cover them with more newspaper or dry towels, and place them in a cool, dark place, such as a drawer, cabinet, or closet. They should dry slowly, protected from light and dust. Let the leaves remain on the stems if you have room, because they will retain more of their natural aromas. You will need the stems of thyme for your *bouquet garni*, and fennel stalks for soup stocks and court bouillons.

Rosemary and bay leaves will dry out naturally in jars or plastic bags. You must be very careful when you dry sage because it often molds and takes on a very disagreeable flavor.

Store dried herbs in tightly sealed jars, away from light and heat. Do not keep for over one year, because they will no longer have any culinary value. Even six months is stretching it.

Freezing Herbs

Most herbs can be frozen. First blanch them in boiling water for 10 seconds, refresh in cold water for 1 minute, and dry between towels. Pack in tablespoon-size portions in plastic and freeze. To use, add before thawed to soups, sauces, vegetable dishes, etc. I do not recommend frozen herbs for salads because they sometimes get slimy upon thawing.

A Glossary of Herbs

Anise

Anise has a distinct liquorice flavor. Its leaves, which look a bit like chervil leaves, bright green and feathery, can be added to salads and cooked vegetables for a nice variation. Its seeds are an important ingredient in Pain d'Epices (page 50) and other spice breads and cakes, and in some biscuits. The herb is an annual that can grow to a height of 2 feet. It likes light, fertile soil and lots of sunlight and heat.

Basil

I have friends in Texas who are so addicted to it that they devote an entire garden every spring to this special herb. I envy them this garden, for I must settle for a small windowpot — although I can find generous bunches daily in my market — and I am almost as fanatical about it as they. It is, I think, my favorite herb. Known in France as "l'Herbe Royale" (its name derives from the Greek "basilikon", which means royal), it was made to accompany tomatoes and pasta, to season Mediterranean vegetable dishes, and will gladly find its way into egg, grain, and cheese dishes, salads, and curries (it grows abundantly in India). It has a pronounced sweet and pungent flavor and is sometimes rather peppery. There are a few varieties of the plant. Most familiar are those with the large, dark green leaves. In the South of France the basil plants are bushy, with very small green leaves; these have a stronger, more anisey flavor than the larger leaf plants. There is also a beautiful variety with purple leaves.

The ultimate basil preparation is *pesto* in Italy, *pistou* in Provence. This is a paste made with large quantities of basil, which is ground together with garlic, pine nuts (for pesto), olive oil, and cheese (Parmesan and Romano in Italy, Gruyère or Parmesan in France). Pesto is served with pasta or vegetables, and Pistou is stirred into a thick minestrone-like soup just before the soup is served.

Common or sweet basil is an annual and can grow to about 3 feet high. It should be started after all danger of frost is past. It grows well in pots and needs lots of sunlight and moisture. If you keep picking off the flowers once they begin to appear, your basil will last well into the autumn.

In France you will often see basil in pots on restaurant terraces. This is because basil is known to ward off flies, which are annoyingly abundant and persistent in Provence. It has always been a tradition for farmers to give the plants as house gifts. A welcome gift indeed, but in my house it wouldn't last very long as an insect repellent.

Bay Leaves

Since antiquity the "Noble Laurel" has been reputed to sharpen the wit of the poet and strengthen the powers of the prophet. It has always symbolized victory on the battle fields and playing fields, and for almost as long its virtues as a culinary herb, just as important, have been widely recognized. The oil of the waxy, dark green leaves of the bay laurel imparts a distinct herbal flavor to soups, stews, vegetable, and bean dishes. I remember vividly the first time I was aware of this taste: I was served lentil soup for the first time at a friend's house, and adored it. I asked my friend's mother what the seasoning was, and she said it was bay leaf. I went right home and requested lentil soup made with bay leaf in it, and have used this herb ever since in stocks, bean dishes, marinades, and many soups. Bay leaves add a rich, subtle flavor to slowly cooked vegetables like artichokes and eggplant. They are an important element in marinades, partly because of their anti-bacterial properties.

Bouquet Garni

A *bouquet garni* consists of one or two sprigs of thyme, one or two sprigs of parsley, and a bay leaf, tied together. Sometimes a stalk of fennel is also included, depending on what you are using it for. It is indispensable in vegetable stocks and stews, imparting a subtle herbal flavor.

Caraway

Caraway, known for its distinctly flavored seeds, is one of those herbs that people either like or detest, so it's best not to serve a dish seasoned with caraway to guests whose tastes are unfamiliar to you. I grew up eating Jewish rye bread with caraway seeds and have always loved the flavor. Not only does it go beautifully with rye, but it is great in potato soups, grain soups, and various salads. Used judiciously it will not dominate a dish but will accent it in a very interesting way. The plant is a biennial and likes sandy soil and full sunlight.

Cayenne

Although often considered a spice, cayenne and the other members of the Capsicum family (the chilis and paprikas) are herbs. It is very high in vitamin C and has several medicinal properties. I take a capsule of it whenever I feel a cold coming on, and it invariably works as a preventative. In the kitchen a small pinch will heighten the flavor of a dish and make something special out of what otherwise might have been a good but not exceptional pot of beans, a soup, or vegetable dish. And not because you and your guests have burnt your mouths. You should be careful never to add too much cayenne, for it is among the hottest of peppers. A pinch is usually sufficient.

Chervil

Chervil has been my most exciting herb discovery since coming to live in France in 1981. Nothing can mimic its sweet, pungent flavor. It is a delicate, feathery plant, a little like flat-leaf parsley in appearance but lighter in color and more fern-like. Its leaves should never be chopped, but plucked from the stems, because chopping bruises the herb and alters its fine, refreshing flavor. Whole strands of chervil add distinction to salads, and the leaves make a particularly elegant garnish for soups, vegetables, eggs, and sauces. It is high in vitamin C and iron and is known to stimulate the appetite.

Chervil is a hardy biennial that grows best when sown in late summer in well-drained, light soil. It will do well in half shade and in window boxes.

Chives

These look like tiny spring onions and are the mildest member of the onion family. A hardy perennial, they are easy to grow, require partial sun and any kind of soil, and should be kept around the kitchen so you can snip them into salads and soups, omelettes and sauces, lightly cooked vegetables, potatoes, herb butters, and fresh cheeses. A lowly pan of scrambled eggs becomes quite special with the addition of chives (page 115). They are high in vitamin C and are one of the *fines herbes*, with chervil, parsley, and tarragon.

Coriander (or Cilantro)

This is an herb I discovered in Mexico, where it is a common ingredient in all sorts of dishes. It is another one of those herbs people either love or hate, and I am someone who loves its strong taste. I first discovered it in the best bowl of beans I'd ever eaten, in a large family restaurant in a Mexican border town. Since then I've never made beans without it; I'm hooked. Mexican or Tex-Mex hot sauce is another food item that cannot exist without cilantro (fresh coriander). I later discovered that this herb is a frequent ingredient in Chinese dishes and curries. It is easy to find in Oriental markets.

Coriander has never been easy for me to grow because it goes to seed very quickly. It likes full sun and chalky soil.

Coriander seeds, whole or ground, have an altogether different flavor.

They are an important seasoning in Greek-style marinated vegetables and ground in curries, spice cakes, and breads. Their flavor is slightly musty and spicy.

Cumin

This is considered by some to be a spice, but I have found it listed in more than one herbal. It has a distinctive, spicy-earthy flavor and is indispensable in curries, many Mexican dishes, and many Middle Eastern dishes. It goes well, whole or ground, with certain cheese and vegetable creations, with potatoes and tofu, and with beans of all kinds. I like it very much with lentils, and I often make a bread seasoned with the whole seeds when I am serving Mexican food.

Dill

When I lived in Austin, Texas, I had a huge dill plant in my front yard that I didn't plant. It was right next to the garbage can, and a seed must have been dumped there and germinated. How lucky I was. I was forever using the versatile herb for my dinners, where I would season different versions of cucumber soups and salads, soups, potato dishes and cabbage dishes and breads with the dill, whose unique, fresh flavor cannot be duplicated.

Dill is widely used in Eastern European and Scandinavian cooking. For that reason I associate it with dishes containing yogurt, cucumbers, potatoes, and cabbage. It is an annual that can grow to a height of about 3 feet, and it looks very much like wild fennel, with tall, hollow stalks and feathery, green leaves. The flavors of the two are not at all similar, however, but they like to cross-pollinate and should never be planted close together.

Dill will grow like a weed from seed, but it must have a well-drained, rich soil and abundant sunshine to thrive.

Dill seeds have a much stronger, saltier flavor than the leaves. They are slightly similar to caraway, though not as strong. I like to add them to breads and cheeses and to tofu spreads, and when ground they make a good salt substitute.

Fennel

Fennel is one of the earliest known herbs. It was discovered in ancient times that it aided in the digestion of oily fish, thus the herb was and still is widely used in fish cookery. Among the Greeks it had the reputation of making fat people lean, and it has always been famous for its good effect on the skin and the eyes.

The anise-flavored, feathery-leafed plant looks like dill and grows like a weed in warm climates. I have seen it on canyon roads in Los Angeles, all over Provence, and along the coast in Britain. Cultivated fennel likes full sun and well-drained soil.

Chopped fresh fennel is a refreshing addition to salads and vegetable dishes and makes a fine garnish for some soups. I like to add it to quiches, and use it sometimes in omelettes and cheese dishes. The seeds are much like anise in flavor, and find their way into Greek-style marinated vegetables, some breads and soups, and other braised vegetable dishes.

Fines Herbes
The *fines herbes* consist of parsley, tarragon, chervil, and chives. Use them in omelettes, cream sauces, cheese spreads, quiches, and salads. Adding *fines herbes* to a dish is like adding a touch of springtime.

Marjoram and Oregano
Marjoram and oregano come from the same family. Oregano is often referred to as "wild marjoram", and indeed, it has a stronger more rustic flavor.

Marjoram has a minty, somewhat thyme-like flavor (it is also called "sweet marjoram"), and is great in salads, soups — especially of the minestrone variety — pizzas, pasta, and vegetable dishes. It is a half-hardy, bushy annual that cannot withstand frost. Its leaves are small, plentiful, and silver-green. The flowers are knotty and purplish and appear at the top of the stem. They have a strong aromatic scent. The plant can grow to a height of 3 feet and is easy to cultivate in pots and window boxes.

Oregano is more rustic than marjoram and more widespread in Southern Europe, where it is found growing wild all over the sunny hillsides. It looks like marjoram but has a stronger, more peppery odor. It too will grow to a height of 3 feet and can be cultivated in pots and window boxes. It likes very well-drained, light soil and lots of sun.

I associate oregano first and foremost with Italian food. A pizza wouldn't be a pizza without it. It was one of the first herbs I ever used, because spaghetti sauce was one of the first things I ever learned to make, and my mother instructed me to add oregano to it. The herb is equally important in many Greek bean dishes and salads, as well as Mediterranean vegetable dishes, eggplant dishes, and hearty soups.

Mint
There are numerous varieties of mint, but the ones used most often in cooking are spearmint and peppermint. I also use apple mint, which has a milder flavor, and pennyroyal, whose tiny leaves are strong and peppery. The recipes in this book are best suited for peppermint.

Once you begin to explore North African and Middle Eastern cuisines you will see how versatile this herb is. It is widely used in these regions in salads, grain dishes, vegetable dishes, and soups. Mint changes the entire aspect of a dish, but used judiciously it will not overpower the other ingredients. The effect is a refreshing one. I often garnish fresh fruit with mint. A tablespoon or two can pick up something as simple as a bowl of sliced oranges and make a really special dessert out of them. It adds an elegant touch to berries, melon, and peaches, too, and blended into fresh orange juice it will make a breakfast drink that will open your eyes much more effectively than a cup of coffee.

Mint grows easily from cuttings in well-watered soil or in pots. It does not need or even like direct sunlight, and requires a good deal of moisture. It spreads quickly, so contain it with bricks or rocks if growing it in your garden. The herb is a very hardy annual.

Parsley
This is the herb with which we are most familiar. The eternal garnish, parsley can go much further than that. It has a slightly bitter flavor and goes well, alone and in combination, with other herbs, with vegetables, grains, legumes, pasta, cheese, and eggs. Middle Eastern and North African recipes often call for large quantities of parsley and here it is quite distinguishable. You find it in abundance in salads, grain dishes, egg dishes, and vegetable and legume combinations.

Parsley is an effective antidote for garlic and onion breath, so serve it with dishes highly seasoned with these ingredients.

The herb comes in several curly varieties, which are what we most often see at supermarkets and greengrocers. But the flat-leafed Italian parsley is actually preferable, for it has a richer, cleaner, more pronounced fragrance. A hardy biennial, it can grow to a height of 2 feet and is easy to cultivate in pots and window boxes. The seeds take a while to germinate. It likes shade and rich, well-worked soil.

Rosemary
This is one of the strongest of the herbs. Its resinous, spiky leaves impart a pungent, savory flavor to Italian and Provençal vegetable dishes, to broiled foods and marinades, where its anti-bacterial properties are as important as its gastronomic virtues. The herb is an evergreen shrub that grows all over Provence and Italy. Because it's so easy to come by in these regions, when I am there I am always adding it to tomato sauces, ratatouilles, vegetables, and bean dishes. The plant can grow to a height of 5 feet and likes light, sandy, fairly dry soil and either full or partial sunlight. It gives off a spicy aroma. I prefer the fresh herb to the dried, not just because of its flavor, but because the leaves of dried rosemary are hard and spiky.

Rosemary seems to have more legends attached to it than any other herb. It goes back thousands of years. It was considered a symbol of immortality by the Greeks and Romans, and was favored for its powers of rejuvenation by the court of Louis XIV.

Rosemary's medicinal virtues are well documented. As an infusion it is a tonic and digestive, stimulating the liver function and circulation. It is excellent for the skin and hair, and its oil makes an effective liniment for sprains, bruises, and gout.

Sage
Another herb with a very distinctive flavor, a little sage goes a long way, and can really make a dish. I shall never forget the spinach and ricotta gnocchi finished in sage butter, which I ate for lunch one day at a small Florentine restaurant. The sage added that special stunning touch that made this dish a truly memorable one. The herb often finds its way into Italian dishes like tomato sauces and slowly simmered vegetable dishes. It is good with pumpkin (a remarkable northern Italian speciality is a pumpkin ravioli with ground almonds, parmesan, and sage), eggplant, and potatoes.

Sage often becomes moldy and takes on an unappetizing musty flavor when dried, so be very careful if drying the herb yourself, and make sure you buy the herb from a reliable source. Dried, it is quite good in stuffings and herb breads.

The plant is a kind of shrub, with thick, long, slender leaves, grey-green, with a pebbly texture. It likes well-drained soil and lots of sunlight.

Sage tea is a good tonic and blood purifier, and the herb is reputed to ensure a long life. The name, in fact, comes from the Latin word *salvare,* to save. Numerous proverbs have been written about its attributes. A Provençal maxim goes:

> Sage Saves
> He who has it in his garden
> Has no need of medicine.

Summer Savory

This is known as "the bean herb" in America, and in the South of France it is used frequently to season fresh goat cheeses. It lends a delicate flavor to beans of all kinds, fresh or dried, and is also used in aromatic sauces. Rather than adding a different flavor of its own, like coriander or cumin, it brings out the flavors of the foods it is cooked with. In this way it makes an excellent substitute for salt.

Summer savory is a bushy annual that can grow to a height of about 1 foot with sparse, dark green leaves along the stems. It likes full sunlight.

One of the reasons that savory has traditionally been added to bean dishes is that it aids in digestion. It has also always had a reputation as an aphrodisiac (its name derives from "satyrus"), which may account for its popularity.

Sorrel

Sorrel is considered both a vegetable and a herb. Used widely in France in soups and purées, alone and with other vegetables, it has been sadly neglected in the United States and Britain. It has a strong acidic flavor, very distinctive and somewhat metallic due to its high oxalic acid content. It should never be cooked in aluminium or metal pots because it oxidizes easily. Sorrel is not only excellent in soups and sauces, but also in egg preparations like omelettes and *oeufs cocottes.*

The leaves of the sorrel plant are broad, oblong, and dark green. They look a little like flat spinach leaves. The plant is very high in vitamins A and C and in iron. It grows well in light, rich soil and in full sunlight. Combine it with spinach, lettuce, and other greens in soups, salads, and purées. It has a strong flavor and a little goes a long way.

When you cook sorrel it will turn a brownish green color upon contact with the heat. The first time I worked with it I kept pulling out leaves, thinking I'd overlooked some bad ones while washing them. When they all turned the same color I realized that this must be normal.

Opposite: Mediterranean Sandwich Loaf (page 116).

Tarragon

French tarragon (avoid Russian tarragon, which is flavorless) is one of the most luxurious of the herbs. Its long, narrow leaves have a unique sweet flavor, somewhat like basil but more tangy, somewhat like anise but not as liquoricey and more bitter. It is very aromatic, essential in Sauce Bearnaise, and is one of the *fines herbes* always welcome in omelettes, quiches, salads, and herb butters and cheeses. A few tablespoons of freshly chopped tarragon will turn an ordinary vegetable broth into a truly elegant soup, perfect for the first course of a rich meal, and even less will make something very special out of a salad.

Tarragon can never be grown from seeds but must be started from cuttings or purchased as small plants. The leaves are bright green and widely spaced on thin stems. The plants need full sun and well-drained soil. The herb is excellent with delicate vegetables like asparagus, peas, and artichokes, and in light cream sauces. It makes a delicious aromatic vinegar and is marvelous, even in its dried state, in vinaigrettes. This is a very useful herb for salt-free diets.

Thyme

Thyme is another one of my favorite herbs. I couldn't be without it, not just for the *bouquet garni* it must be part of, for seasoning soup stocks, beans, and sauces, but for the distinct, tangy touch its tiny green leaves add to vegetable and cheese dishes, soups, and salads. It is so distinguishable that a little goes a long way, and it is because of this unmistakable flavor that I love it so much. It is delicate and earthy at the same time. Dried thyme is an important ingredient in herb breads and bean pâtés, and also savory bean dishes and soups.

Garden thyme can grow to about 12 inches and is a perennial evergreen bush. Lemon thyme is a creeper and is most suitable in rock gardens. Like rosemary, it grows all over Provence and Italy, and I grew accustomed to running out and picking it for one dish or another every time I cooked when I lived in the South of France.

The thymes like chalky, fertile soil and full sunlight. They spread quickly.

HONEY

I will never forget the first time I walked out into the lavender fields behind the farmhouse I have summered in, in Provence. I was immediately deafened by the buzzing of thousands of bees. At first I panicked and wanted to run. Then I realized that these bees had no interest in me; they were frantically gathering up nectar from the deep purple flowers, nectar which would soon become the inimitable lavender honey I stirred into my tea every morning.

At the time I was unaware of the miraculous process that the manufacture of honey by bees is. Their labor and organization is so phenomenal that it is worth sketching here.

Bees live in highly regimented colonies consisting of only one fertile female, the "queen", and anywhere from 50,000 to 60,000 "subjects". The queen bee has one purpose in life, to lay eggs — about 200,000 a year — between the months of February and September. She lives four to five years and produces fewer eggs in later life. For this reason bee-keepers usually replace her with a younger queen before she dies. Nature endows the queen with a hormone called "pheromone"; this is her blue blood, for pheromone prevents the other females in the colony, called workers, from ovulating, thus assuring her the crown. It also serves in protecting the hive, for whenever there is danger the queen releases the hormone and it puts the other bees on the alert.

A male bee serves no other function than to fertilize the queen; this is followed by a sure and cruel death, as he falls to the ground, ripped asunder, his sexual organ left inside the queen. The males that have followed the queen out of the hive and have not been quick enough to fertilize her go back to the hive but are immediately chased out by the workers. They soon die among the flowers, for they have neither the equipment for gathering nectar nor stingers for their protection. Theirs is a sad lot.

The workers are highly disciplined within the hive. Some take care of the cells where the queen will lay her eggs, others nourish the larvae with the "royal jelly" with which nature has endowed them, others guard the hive, and the rest gather and transport nectar. Their lifespan is five to six weeks, and it is during the last two weeks of their lives that they leave the hive to search for flowers.

To collect a pound of honey bees must fly a distance equivalent to two to three orbits of the earth, visiting up to a million flowers. When they find flowers they return to the hive, where they perform a miraculous and elaborate dance in order to communicate the whereabouts and scent of the nectar. A dance of concentric circles, so many to the right and so many to the left, indicates that the flowers are relatively close by. A more frenetic kind of movement indicates that the fields are further away, usually two or three miles. With that information, swarms of bees now leave the hives to go and gather up nectar.

Nectar is a sugary liquid contained in specific glands of flowers. Bees extract it with a proboscis which extends from their hairy tongues, and store it in a special abdominal pouch. A bee must pump 1,000 to 1,500 flowers to fill this pocket. It is hard work, but she can also eat some of the nectar to nourish herself while she is at it. As soon as the nectar is in its sack, enzymes begin to change its saccarose to glucose and levulose; the honey-making process has begun. When the bees return to the hive they regurgitate the nectar, which is passed along to the other bees in long strands of droplets. The bees then form long lines and furiously bat their wings to produce air currents which will evaporate a large portion of the water contained in the nectar. The last step involves swallowing the nectar again, ruminating for awhile, then placing it in the beehive cells, which they seal with wax. This is what they will live on all winter long.

Bee-keepers gather the honey by removing the wax honeycombs, arranged in man-made beehives in neat shelves, and spinning them in a centrifugal apparatus, which draws the honey from the cells. The honey is then strained two or three times to remove impurities, and packed in jars.

Because of the bees' elaborate system of communication, swarms return to the same fields for days on end, and will only gather one kind of nectar at a time. Since bee-keepers know the seasons and whereabouts of the different kinds of flowers, they can be sure of the source of their honey.

Honey vs. Sugar

How many times have I listened to and participated in arguments over the virtues of honey over sugar? I have always avoided sugar in my cooking and substituted honey, not because honey is really less fattening than sugar, for it is a sugar and should be eaten in moderation, but because it is a less concentrated form of sugar and is easier for the body to assimilate. Sugar is so refined that the warning signals which would normally prevent us from eating too much of it are no longer present. There is a natural "gag factor" in honey, as there is in other highly concentrated sweets like dried fruit. We begin to feel sick before we've eaten too much.

But beyond the nutritional considerations, honey is a gastronomic treasure and has been valued by cooks and eaters for centuries. It is not just a sweetener, but a seasoning like herbs or spices, which can add character to many savory dishes, soups, vegetables, salads, and sauces, as well as desserts.

Nutritional Information

Honey is heavier than sugar and has a higher liquid content, so it cannot be substituted measure for measure. A teaspoon of honey has more calories than a teaspoon of sugar because it weighs more. But it is also sweeter, so you need less than a teaspoon to get the same sweetening effect. Gram for gram honey is actually less calorific.

Composition: 100 grams honey
Calories: 304 (100 grams of sugar contains 400 calories.)

Fructose	38.2 g*
Glucose	31.3 g*
Water	17.2 g
Sucrose	1.3 g
Phosphate	16 mg
Potassium	10 mg
Magnesium	6 mg
Sodium	5 mg
Sulphate	5 mg
Iron	0.5 mg
Copper	0.2 mg
Manganese	0.2 mg

Trace amounts of nicotinic acid, pantothenic acid, pyridoxin, riboflavin, thiamin, biotin, folic acid, ascorbic acid, enzymes, and trace lipids.

* The proportions of these sugars vary in different honeys.

Cooking with Honey

The most important thing to remember when using honey in cookery is that it has a high liquid content, and compensation must be made by slightly reducing the other liquids in the recipe. Also it is best, when possible, to add honey towards the end of the cooking to avoid altering its flavor.

— One cup (8 fluid ounces) of honey weighs 12 ounces. The measures in this collection, however, will be in liquid measures.

— To substitute honey for sugar in a given recipe, reduce the amount of sweetener called for by at least one-fourth (up to a half, according to your taste), and reduce the liquid in the recipe by one-eighth.

— Most cakes, with the exception of spice breads and some dense honey cakes, do not adapt well to honey. It is too heavy, and your cakes will be dense, with no fine crumb. It does, however, give breads a good texture and a longer shelf life. When baking with honey be careful not to overheat your oven — 400°F to 425°F — because honey will darken and caramelize quickly.

— Honey foams dramatically when it reaches boiling point, so use a large saucepan for syrups.

— To facilitate measuring, oil or butter measuring spoons and cups (this way it won't stick), and heat solid honey gently in a *bain marie* (see section on Consistency, page 23).

— Honey is at its peak flavor when freshly harvested, so the autumn is the best time to sample and purchase it.

Storing Honey

Honey will keep in a well-sealed jar for up to two years if stored in a cool, dark place. Once opened it is best to consume it fairly quickly, although it still has a long life. Do not refrigerate, and do not keep in a warm cupboard. If the honey develops a foamy surface it has turned, and should be thrown out.

The Different Kinds of Honeys

When I went to Harrods in London and La Maison du Miel in Paris to look at the different kinds of honeys I was astounded. There were well over forty different kinds of honeys at each store. Harrods had about fifteen kinds of English honey from various producers, plus imported honeys from France, Greece, Canada, Rumania, Australia, Tasmania, Hungary, New Zealand, Israel, Spain, Mexico, Chile, Guatemala, Jamaica, and the South Pacific. At La Maison du Miel in Paris there were varieties from a dozen regions of France, plus many imported honeys.

Honey can be divided into two types: those made from one flower, and those originating from several. The unifloral honeys are like "crus" of wine, and have distinctive flavors depending on the flowers; some are very mild, some perfumed and floral, others strong, even acrid. The multifloral honeys vary in strength and character according to the flowers from which they originate. They can be quite refined, if they come from, say, lavender and other mild summer flowers, or they can be strong mountain honeys.

Whether unifloral or multifloral, color is the best way to judge the character of a honey. The light, limpid honeys are the mildest, the dark ones are strong. For all-purpose cooking and sweetening, the lighter honeys are the best, as they won't dominate whatever they are going into. However, these honeys would be lost in spicy dishes and pastries like "Pain d'Epices" or spice cakes, so if you intend to make these, have stronger honeys on hand.

I have listed the most commonly stocked honeys below and have categorized them as Mild, Medium, and Strong, which is how they will be listed in the recipes.

Mild Honeys

These are honeys whose flavors are not highly pronounced, though each is distinctive and some are quite floral and aromatic. They are all good for baking, for sweetening teas and spreading on bread or toast, and for cooking wherever a strong honey taste is not desired. Do not waste them on spice breads and cakes, for their subtle flavors will be lost.

Acacia. This is the king of the honeys. Of all of them, its flavor is the least pronounced, almost like a sugar syrup. It is a light, clear liquid which hardly ever crystallizes. Most acacia honey comes from Hungary, and some from France.

Clover. The next mildest, after acacia. This is slightly darker in color, though still very light, and can be either liquid or thick and slightly solid. It has a very agreeable waxy taste, as if it were just extracted from the hive. Clover honey always tastes like springtime to me.

Colza (Colza or Rape). This is a very thick, almost ivory-colored honey, very sweet and creamy. It looks like a light-colored wax, and because of its texture makes a delicious spread. It is quite good mixed with butter. Because it crystallizes quickly you will have to heat it for cooking.

English Honeys (Except heather). Most of the English honeys I tasted, those I found at Harrods, were clover and blossom honeys with a light color and a very sweet, sometimes slightly acidic but not pronounced flavor. They are less mild than the acacia and colza but could easily be put to the same uses. There were over eight kinds at Harrods, and the only really strong English honey I tasted was heather (see listing in next category).

Hyacinth or **Bluebell.** The hyacinth I tasted was imported from Australia and had a thick creamy consistency, a fairly light color and a very agreeable, perfumed flavor. It tastes like a very slightly caramelized thick syrup, a little like butterscotch, and is particularly good spread on bread.

Lavender. This is another aristocrat of honeys, with its unmatched floral, slightly acidic, aromatic taste. It is liquid when just gathered but quickly thickens, without becoming grainy. It has an amber color and is particularly good in teas and on bread.

Rosemary. I find the French rosemary and Spanish rosemary honeys different. The French variety is lighter in color, a pale yellow to amber, and not quite as pronounced as the Spanish, which is more amber, with a slightly musty overtone. Nevertheless they are both unassuming, very sweet and fruity, good in sweet and sour dishes, pungent dishes, and teas.

Sunflower. This also has an unassuming flavor, though more pronounced than acacia. The golden yellow, sometimes amber honey has a sweet though discreet perfume and a fine, sometimes creamy or grainy texture.

Thistle. Much like colza, with which it is often combined, this honey has a very sweet taste, a creamy consistency, and practically an ivory color. A favorite among French children, it is marvelous on bread or toast and as a sweetener for tea.

Toutes Fleurs. These multifloral honeys will depend on the flowers from which they originate, but I have found enough light-colored, thick, mild variations to list Toutes Fleurs here. There are also several dark, stronger varieties. The color will be the indicator.

Medium Honeys

These are not strong, but their flavors are pronounced enough to avoid using them in dishes where there is a great deal of honey, like a custard or a *Creme Anglaise,* or a honey cake without spices. They are fine in breads, where honey is called for in relatively small quantities, and in teas or on bread or toast. You *will* taste them, but they are not overbearing like the honeys in the next section.

Australian Strawberry Clover. I found this honey at Harrods. It is not as mild as the other clover honeys, but has a fruitier, more highly perfumed flavor, like the orange blossom honeys.

Lime Blossom Honey. This, from Rumania, has a citrus flavor, slightly pronounced, and an amber color.

Orange Blossom Honey. This has an orange-amber color and a highly perfumed, fruity flavor. I used it all the time in Texas, where citrus abounds, but found it was too strong for subtle dishes.

South Pacific. I found this at Harrods also. It is dark and has a caramel flavor. It's quite agreeable and would be good in or on breads.

Strong Honeys

These are almost all dark in color (the lightest are heather — "bruyère" in French — and chestnut — "chataigner" in French), and fairly caustic. They should be used for spice breads and spice cakes, where the taste of a milder honey would be lost.

Blue Gum Tree (from Australia). This has a syrupy, sorghum-like taste and golden brown color.

Buckwheat. Very strong and dark. This can be used in small amounts in breads and pancakes that call for buckwheat flour.

Chestnut. This has a dark golden color, though not as dark as the other strong honeys, and when it crystallizes it takes on a yellower hue. It has a strong, slightly bitter flavor.

Fir (Fr. Sapin). This usually comes from the mountainous regions of France and is one of the strongest honeys. It is dark brown, sometimes almost black, and stays liquid for a long time. It should be used with caution as its flavor can be quite overbearing.

Heather. This has a pronounced flavor and can be very caustic, enough to irritate the throat. But it is not always this strong, and I have found some French heather honey with a deep cherry-like flavor.

Montaigne. Mountain honeys from France, whether from the Alps, the Jura, or Vosges, are almost always dark, resinous, and strong.

Thyme, including **Hymettus honey from Greece.** The Greeks were known for their aromatic honey, gathered from the thyme on Mount Hymettus. There are several varieties of thyme honey. They are amber to dark brown, and their consistencies vary from thick and syrupy to pasty. The flavor is always pronounced and sometimes a bit piquant. Thyme honeys can be used in spice breads and in sweet-and-sour dishes.

Tilleul (Linden Tree). This is another fairly dark, spicy honey. It is not, however, acrid, and is suitable for sweetening tea or spreading on bread, as well as sweetening spice breads. It is very sweet, with a sometimes creamy, sometimes grainy consistency.

Consistency

Most honey eventually thickens or crystallizes, due to the presence of glucose crystals, dust, and pollens. The honeys which remain liquid, like acacia, have a higher proportion of levulose. Whether a honey is solid or liquid has no bearing on its quality (unless it has been boiled, like some commercial manufacturers do in the United States, robbing the honey of its flavor and nutrients), although I have sometimes noticed that the taste of a honey will change when it solidifies. Lavender honey, for example, has a slightly more acidic flavor in its liquid state than in its solid state.

It is easier to cook with honey when it is liquid, and all honeys can be rendered liquid by gently heating them in the jar in a pan of simmering water. As long as you do not boil the honey you will not alter its food value or perfume. Overheating honey, on the other hand, destroys its flavors and its vitamins. In some of the recipes in this book, however (those for the syrups and sherbets), the honey must be brought to the boiling point, but it needn't be cooked to death.

Always look for pure, unadulterated honey, whether multifloral or unifloral. Some of the large commercial manufacturers feed bees on sugar water and filter and boil the honey until it has very little character and no nutrients.

CHAPTER I

BREAKFASTS

Banana-Yogurt Breakfast Drink

Makes 1 drink

1 cup plain low-fat yogurt
1 teaspoon mild honey
Juice of 1 orange, or ¼ cup apple juice
1 small banana
2 teaspoons brewers yeast
1 tablespoon toasted wheat germ
1 or 2 ice cubes

Place all ingredients in a blender and blend until smooth.

Braided Fruit-Filled Coffee Cake

For the dough:

1 tablespoon active dry yeast

½ cup lukewarm water

½ cup orange juice

4 tablespoons mild honey

1 egg, beaten

4 tablespoons powdered milk

1 tablespoon grated orange rind

2½ cups unbleached white flour

3 tablespoons melted butter or safflower oil

1 teaspoon sea salt

1½ cups whole wheat flour

Additional unbleached white flour for kneading

For the filling:

¼ cup water, plus more as needed

½ cup chopped, dried fruit

2 peaches, peeled and sliced

3 plums, sliced

2 apples, sliced

1 banana, sliced

½ cup chopped almonds

1 teaspoon ground cinnamon

¼ teaspoon freshly grated nutmeg

1 tablespoon grated orange rind

1 teaspoon vanilla extract

4 tablespoons mild honey

For the topping:

1 egg, beaten with 4 tablespoons water

½ cup slivered almonds

	4-8 tablespoons mild honey
	½ cup water

1. Prepare dough. Dissolve yeast in water in a large bowl. Heat orange juice in a small pan and stir in honey, then remove from heat and cool to lukewarm. Add to yeast mixture. Stir in egg, powdered milk, and orange rind. Stir in ⅔ cup of the unbleached white flour and stir 100 times for the sponge. Cover and set in a warm place 1 hour.
2. Fold in butter or oil and salt. Fold in whole wheat flour and remaining unbleached white flour. Flour kneading surface and turn out dough. Knead 10 to 15 minutes, until smooth and elastic, adding flour as necessary. Wash out the bowl, oil it, and place dough in it. Cover and let rise in a warm place 1 hour.
3. Meanwhile prepare the filling. Combine water and dried fruit in a saucepan and simmer over medium heat, adding water if necessary, until fruit is softened. Combine with all the other filling ingredients except honey in a large bowl, and toss together well.
4. Punch down dough and turn out onto your work surface. Roll into a rectangle about 16 inches long and 12 inches wide. Brush with honey, and spread filling down the center third of rectangle. Now, using a sharp knife, cut dough on either side into 1-inch strips pointed in a downward angle.
5. Fold strips in over filling, alternating sides so that you are weaving one over the other like a braid. When you get to the end, pinch braids over lower end. Carefully transfer coffee cake to a lightly oiled baking sheet. Let rise 40 minutes while you preheat oven to 350°F.
6. Brush braid with egg wash, sprinkle with slivered almonds, and brush again with egg wash. Place in preheated oven and bake 30 to 40 minutes, or until golden brown.
7. While coffee cake is baking, combine remaining honey with water in a saucepan and heat together. When you remove coffee cake from oven, brush with this mixture.
8. Serve warm.

Illustrated opposite page 32.

Peanut Butter Tofu Spread

Safflower oil for baking dish
½ pound tofu
5 tablespoons plain low-fat yogurt
3-4 tablespoons mild honey, or to taste
1 large or 2 small bananas
2-3 tablespoons unsalted peanut butter, to taste
½ teaspoon cinnamon
½ teaspoon nutmeg
1 teaspoon vanilla
1 tablespoon lemon juice
2 teaspoons whole wheat flour

1. Preheat oven to 350°F. Lightly oil a small baking dish or a 1 quart casserole.
2. Blend all the ingredients together until smooth. Pour into baking dish and bake 30 to 40 minutes, or until firm and just beginning to brown. Remove from oven, cool, and chill.

Note: This will keep for a week in the refrigerator. It does not freeze.

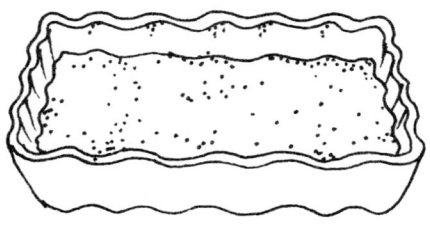

Couscous with Honey and Fruit

Serves 4

1 cup couscous
2 cups water
1 tablespoon butter
1 apple, cored and chopped
1 pear, cored and chopped
3 tablespoons water or apple juice
1 tablespoon honey
4 tablespoons raisins
1 teaspoon ground cinnamon
½ tablespoon freshly grated nutmeg
Plain low-fat yogurt and additional honey for topping

1. Place couscous in a bowl and pour on water. Let sit 10 to 15 minutes, or until soft.
2. Heat butter in a frying pan and add apple and pear. Sauté a few minutes, then add water or apple juice, honey, raisins, and spices. Cook, stirring over medium heat, 3 to 5 minutes.
3. Stir in couscous and heat through, stirring. Remove from heat and serve, topping with yogurt, and if you wish, additional honey.

Oatmeal with Fruit and Honey

Serves 4

2 cups water
2 tablespoons mild honey
Pinch of sea salt
1 cup rolled oats
3 tablespoons raisins
½-1 teaspoon ground cinnamon
½ teaspoon freshly grated nutmeg
1 apple, grated and tossed with juice of ½ lemon
Warm milk for topping
Additional cinnamon (optional)

1. Place water in a saucepan, add honey and salt, and bring to a rolling boil.
2. Slowly pour in rolled oats, stirring all the while with a wooden spoon. Add raisins, cinnamon, and nutmeg, bring to a second boil, and reduce heat. Cover and simmer 15 to 20 minutes, or until liquid is absorbed.
3. Top each serving with grated apple, warm milk, and if you wish, additional cinnamon.

Minted Breakfast Drink
Makes 1 drink

A marvelous, refreshing drink to wake up to.

1 cup freshly squeezed orange juice
2 tablespoons fresh mint
Handful of alfalfa sprouts
½ ripe banana
2 ice cubes

Place all ingredients in a blender and blend until smooth. Drink at once.

Pain Perdu (French Toast)

Serves 6

French toast is traditionally made with stale brioche, the French solution to leftover bread. I often use day-old challah (see recipe page 42), but you can really use any bread, and it doesn't have to be stale. It should end up crisp on the outside and soft and custardy on the inside. The honey you use can be strong or mild.

1 loaf challah or other bread, cut in ¾-inch slices
3 large eggs
1 cup milk
¾ teaspoon vanilla extract
1 tablespoon honey
Pinch of cinnamon
Pinch of freshly grated nutmeg
1 teaspoon orange flower water (optional)
Small pinch of sea salt
Unsalted butter for sautéing, as needed
Additional honey for topping

1. Slice bread an hour or two before you make the French toast, if you can, so that it will dry out.
2. Put oven on low (unless intending to serve as soon as cooked). Beat eggs with milk and stir in vanilla, honey, cinnamon, nutmeg, optional orange flower water, and salt. Heat butter in a large, heavy frying pan over low heat.
3. Dip bread slices into batter on both sides. They should be saturated but not so soggy that they fall apart. Place in frying pan and continue dipping slices and adding them to pan (but don't overcrowd the pan). Sauté slowly, until the first side turns golden brown, about 5 to 7 minutes. Then turn and sauté on the other side until golden brown. Place in oven on a baking sheet to keep warm if you aren't serving at once. Serve with honey.

Opposite: Braided Fruit-Filled Coffee Cake (page 26).

Mixed Grains Muesli

Makes 3 servings

> 1 cup water
> 1 cup milk (or use all water)
> Pinch of sea salt
> ½ cup rolled oats
> ½ cup wheat flakes
> 2 tablespoons bran
> 1 teaspoon cinnamon
> 3 tablespoons raisins
> ½ apple, grated or finely chopped
> ½ pear, grated or finely chopped
> 2-4 tablespoons toasted wheat germ
> 1 tablespoon honey
> Additional warm milk to taste
> 2 tablespoons broken pecans or chopped hazelnuts

1. Bring water and milk to a boil in a 1 quart saucepan. Add a little salt.
2. Combine oats, wheat, bran, and cinnamon, stirring all the while with a wooden spoon; add this very slowly to boiling liquid. Stir in raisins and when liquid reaches a second boil, cover, reduce heat, and simmer gently 15 minutes, or until liquid is absorbed.
3. Spoon into bowls and top with wheat germ, grated apples and pears, honey, and pecans. Add warm milk to taste.

Fancy Granola

Enough to fill a gallon jar

If you make this large amount you'll only have to make granola once a month or even less — unless of course you find it so good (as you undoubtedly will) that you also eat it for snacks. This makes a nice gift as well as an important family staple.

3 cups rolled oats
1½ cups flaked wheat
1½ cups flaked rye
3 cups raw wheat germ
1 cup soy flour
¼ cup powdered milk
1 teaspoon sea salt
1 tablespoon cinnamon
2 teaspoons nutmeg
⅔ cup sunflower seeds
⅔ cup chopped almonds
⅔ cup cashews
⅔ cup sesame seeds, cracked in a blender
⅔ cup grated or shaved coconut
2 tablespoons vanilla extract
¼ cup milk
¾ cup safflower oil
1 cup mild honey
2 cups raisins

1. Preheat oven to 325°F.
2. In a large bowl mix together all the dry ingredients except raisins. Add vanilla and milk.
3. Heat honey and oil together over low heat in a saucepan, just until they blend together easily. Pour mixture over granola and stir and fold in so that all the grains are coated. Make sure that no part of the mixture is dry, or granola won't bake evenly.
4. Oil or butter two large baking pans and spoon in granola. The layers should not be more than 1½ inches thick. Place in oven and set timer for 15

minutes. Stir mixture and set for another 15 minutes. Stir again. After 45 minutes granola should be brown (it may be done a little sooner, so check carefully after the first 30 minutes). Now stir in raisins and turn off heat. Leave oven door ajar and let cool in oven.

5. When granola is completely cool, spoon into jars or plastic bags. If possible, store in refrigerator.

Morning Tofu Spread

This is nice to have on hand to spread on toast in the morning.

½ pound tofu
¼ cup plain yogurt
2 small apples
2-3 tablespoons mild honey
2 tablespoons lemon juice
½ teaspoon cinnamon
¼ teaspoon nutmeg
1 tablespoon sesame tahini
½-1 teaspoon vanilla, to taste
2 teaspoons whole wheat pastry flour

1. Preheat oven to 350°F and bake apples until completely soft. Core apples and set aside.
2. Oil or butter a loaf pan or 1 quart casserole. Keep oven on.
3. Blend all ingredients including baked, cored apples together until completely smooth in a blender or food processor and pour into prepared baking dish. Bake 30 to 40 minutes, or until firm and just beginning to brown. Cool and refrigerate. Spread on bread or toast.

Note: This will last a week in the refrigerator, well wrapped.

Strawberry Omelette

This may sound unlikely, but it's one of the most special breakfasts I can think of. Makes a particularly memorable breakfast in bed.

For each omelette:

1 tablespoon butter for pan

2 eggs, beaten

A generous handful of stemmed strawberries

2 tablespoons plain yogurt

1 teaspoon mild honey

Fresh mint for garnish

1. Heat butter in an omelette pan, and meanwhile beat eggs.
2. Crush strawberries very slightly and mix together with yogurt and honey.
3. When butter has stopped sizzling, pour in eggs and tilt pan to coat evenly. Gently shake pan while lifting edges of omelette so that uncooked eggs can run underneath. As soon as it is set, spread strawberry mixture down the center.
4. Fold omelette, cook a minute longer, and turn out of pan onto a plate. Garnish with fresh mint and serve.

Honeyed Yogurt Cereal Topping

Try this for a change on hot cereal or granola.

1 cup plain low-fat yogurt

1 tablespoon mild honey

½ ripe banana

½ teaspoon vanilla extract

Pinch of nutmeg

Blend together all ingredients in a blender or food processor until smooth. Refrigerate until ready to use.

Semolina with Raisins and Cinnamon

Serves 4

2½ cups water
¼ teaspoon sea salt
1 cup semolina or cream of wheat
1 teaspoon cinnamon
4 tablespoons raisins
1 cup Honeyed Yogurt Cereal Topping (page 36)

1. Bring water to a boil in a saucepan. Add salt, and slowly pour in semolina in a very thin stream, stirring all the time with a wooden spoon.
2. Add sea salt, cinnamon, and raisins, bring to a second boil, reduce heat, and cover. Cook 15 minutes, or until liquid is absorbed.
3. Serve, topping each bowl with a generous amount of Honeyed Yogurt Cereal Topping.

Buckwheat Pancakes

Makes 18 pancakes

2 eggs, separated
2 tablespoons honey*
1 cup milk
1 tablespoon melted butter or safflower oil
¾ cup sifted whole wheat pastry flour
¾ cup sifted buckwheat flour
¼ teaspoon sea salt
1 teaspoon baking powder
Oil for sautéing
Honey for topping

1. Beat together egg yolks, honey, milk, and melted butter or safflower oil.
2. Sift together whole wheat pastry flour and buckwheat flour, sea salt, and baking powder.
3. Stir egg yolk mixture into flour mixture.
4. Beat egg whites until they form stiff, shiny peaks. Gently fold into batter.
5. Heat a heavy, wide frying pan over medium-high heat and brush with oil. Drop in heaping tablespoons of batter. Cook on the first side until bubbles break through, turn (it should be golden brown), and cook until golden brown on the other side. Serve warm, with honey.

* You can use mild or strong honey. Buckwheat honey, which is dark and strong, would give these a pronounced buckwheat flavor. Experiment with different kinds.

Yogurt Pancakes

Makes 18 pancakes

2 eggs, separated
1 tablespoon honey
1 cup plain yogurt
1 tablespoon melted butter or safflower oil
1½ cups sifted whole wheat pastry flour
Pinch of sea salt
1 teaspoon baking powder
Oil for sautéing
Honey for topping

1. Beat together egg yolks, honey, yogurt, and melted butter or safflower oil.
2. Sift together flour, salt, and baking powder.
3. Stir egg yolk mixture into flour mixture.
4. Beat egg whites until they form stiff, shiny peaks. Gently fold into batter.
5. Heat a heavy, wide frying pan over medium-high heat and brush with oil. Drop batter in by heaping tablespoons. Cook on the first side until bubbles break through, turn (it should be golden brown), and cook until golden brown on the other side. Serve warm, with honey.

CHAPTER II

BREADS

Oatmeal, Cornmeal, and Honey Bread

Makes 2 loaves

2 cups lukewarm water
1 tablespoon active dry yeast
1 cup plain yogurt
4 tablespoons mild honey
2 cups unbleached white flour
2 cups whole wheat flour
1 tablespoon sea salt
4 tablespoons safflower oil
2 cups rolled oats
1 cup cornmeal
2 cups whole wheat flour
Additional 2 cups whole wheat or unbleached white flour for kneading*
1 egg, for glaze

1. Dissolve yeast in water in a large bowl. Stir in honey and yogurt, and gradually whisk in the first 2 cups unbleached white flour, then the first 2 cups whole wheat flour. Stir 100 times, then cover bowl with plastic wrap or a damp towel, and place in a warm spot to rise for 1 hour, or until bubbling.
2. Fold in salt and oil, then oats and cornmeal. Begin adding whole wheat flour, and when you can turn dough out of bowl place a cup of flour on your kneading surface and turn out dough. Knead 10 minutes, adding flour as necessary. When dough is stiff and elastic, oil bowl and place dough in it seam side up first, then seam side down. Cover and leave in a warm place to rise 1 to 1½ hours, or until doubled in size.
3. Punch down dough and turn out onto a floured surface. Knead a few times, then divide dough in half and form 2 loaves. Place in oiled breadpans, upside down first, then rightside up, cover, and set aside to rise 1 hour, or until bread comes above edges of pans. During the last 15 minutes of rising, preheat oven to 375°F.
4. Lightly brush loaves with beaten egg, place in oven, and bake 45 to 55 minutes, or until golden and they respond to tapping with a hollow sound. Remove from oven and pans and cool on a rack.

*If your flour is very coarse and heavy, use unbleached white flour or find a lighter whole wheat pastry flour.

Note: This bread freezes well. Double wrap in plastic wrap and foil or plastic wrap and a plastic bag.

Holiday Challah

Makes 2 braided loaves

1 cup milk
½ cup lukewarm water
1 tablespoon active dry yeast
3 tablespoons mild honey
1 teaspoon vanilla
½ teaspoon mace
½ teaspoon ground cardamom
3 eggs, beaten
2 tablespoons grated orange rind
4 to 5 cups unbleached white flour
4 tablespoons safflower oil or melted butter
2 teaspoons sea salt
1 cup wheat germ
2 cups whole wheat flour
½ cup currants
½ cup chopped walnuts
Additional unbleached white flour for kneading
1 egg, beaten with 4 tablespoons water, for egg wash
Poppy seeds

1. Scald milk and cool to lukewarm.
2. Dissolve yeast in lukewarm water, and when milk has cooled to lukewarm, stir in along with honey, vanilla, mace, cardamom, eggs, and orange rind. Add 3 cups of the unbleached white flour, a cup at a time, to make a sponge. Stir 100 times, cover, and set in a warm place 1 hour.
3. When hour is up, fold in oil or butter and sea salt, then wheat germ and whole wheat flour. When dough comes away from sides of bowl, place a cup of unbleached white flour on your kneading surface and turn out dough. Knead until dough is stiff and elastic and somewhat silky, adding more unbleached white flour as necessary.
4. Wash out bowl, oil, and set dough in it to rise for 1 to 1½ hours.

BREADS

5. Punch down dough and turn out onto work surface, which you should flour lightly. Knead in currants and walnuts, then divide dough into 6 equal pieces for 2 braided loaves (or you can make 4 to 6 miniature loaves), weighing the pieces to make sure they are equal. Roll each piece out into a rectangle about 9 inches long, then roll up into a tight cylinder. Roll each cylinder on the work surface until 12 to 14 inches long. Attach 3 cylinders by pinching the ends together. Fold pinched part under and make a braid; pinch together at the other end and fold under. Place braids on an oiled baking sheet and brush with oil. Let rise in a warm place 30 minutes.

6. Towards the end of the rising time, preheat oven to 375°F. Brush braids with egg wash, sprinkle with poppy seeds, and brush with egg wash again. Bake 40 minutes, brushing again with egg wash halfway through. Cool on a rack.

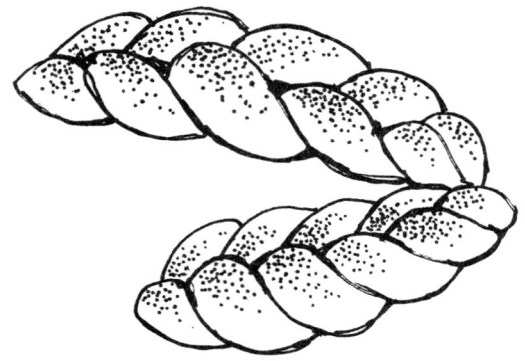

Fig and Walnut Bread

Makes 2 loaves

For the dough:

1½ cups milk

6 tablespoons unsalted butter

½ cup mild honey

2 scant teaspoons sea salt

2 tablespoons active dry yeast

½ cup lukewarm water

2 eggs, at room temperature

5 cups whole wheat flour

Up to 3 cups unbleached white flour

For the filling:

3 tablespoons honey

3 tablespoons unsalted butter

2 teaspoons cinnamon

1 teaspoon ground cloves

1-1½ cups chopped, dried figs

1 cup finely chopped walnuts

For the glaze:

1 egg, beaten with the remaining honey-butter mixture or with ¼ cup water

1. Combine milk, butter, and honey for the dough along with salt in a saucepan and heat together until butter is melted. Stir together to dissolve honey, and set aside until lukewarm.
2. Dissolve yeast in the ½ cup lukewarm water in a large mixing bowl.
3. When milk mixture has cooled, beat in eggs and add to dissolved yeast. Begin stirring in whole wheat flour, a cup at a time. After you have added about 4 cups, stir vigorously 100 times. Add remaining whole wheat flour, fold in, and add a cup of unbleached white flour. By the time you fold this in, the dough should be ready to turn out onto kneading surface.
4. Place some unbleached flour on board and scrape out all the dough.

BREADS

Begin kneading, adding flour as necessary, and knead about 10 minutes, or until dough is stiff and elastic.

5. Oil bowl and place dough in it, rounded side down first, then rounded side up. Cover with plastic wrap or a towel and place in a warm spot to rise for 1½ hours, or until doubled in bulk.
6. Meanwhile prepare your ingredients for the filling. Finely chop walnuts and figs; combine in a bowl. Melt butter and honey together in a small bowl, and stir in cinnamon and cloves.
7. Punch down dough and turn out onto a lightly floured kneading surface. Divide into 2 pieces and knead each into a ball. Let rest 10 minutes.
8. Roll out each piece of dough into a rectangle, about 11 × 8 inches. Brush with honey-butter mixture, then sprinkle with nuts and figs, dividing mixture evenly between the two breads. Leave a 1-inch border around the edge of flattened dough. Roll up dough like a Swiss roll, fold ends in, and pinch all the seams together.
9. Oil breadpans generously and place dough in pans, seam side down. Cover and place in a warm spot to rise 1 hour. Then 20 minutes before the end of the rising, preheat oven to 400°F.
10. Beat egg in bowl in which you melted butter and honey. Brush loaves and place in oven. After 10 minutes turn the heat down to 350°F. Bake another 40 minutes, brushing again with egg wash halfway through the baking. Loaves should be golden brown and respond to tapping with a hollow sound.
11. Remove from heat. To unmold it may be necessary to run a butter knife around the inside edges of the pan. Remove from pans and cool on a rack.

Note: This can be frozen. Once thawed it will dry out fairly rapidly.

Dill and Cottage Cheese Casserole Bread

Makes 1 loaf

4 tablespoons lukewarm water
1 tablespoon active dry yeast
1 teaspoon honey
8 ounces large curd cottage cheese, at room temperature
1 egg, at room temperature
1 tablespoon grated onion
2 tablespoons safflower oil
1½ teaspoons sea salt
¼ teaspoon baking soda
3 tablespoons chopped, fresh dill
¼ cup soy flour
2 cups whole wheat flour
½ to 1 cup unbleached white flour

1. Dissolve yeast and honey in warm water in a large mixing bowl and allow to sit 10 to 15 minutes, or until it bubbles.
2. Press cottage cheese through a sieve, or purée in a food processor fitted with the steel blade. Stir into yeast mixture, and beat in egg. Add onion, oil, salt, baking soda, dill, and soy flour and stir well.
3. Gradually stir in whole wheat flour. Place about 2 handfuls of unbleached flour on kneading surface and turn out dough. Knead 5 to 10 minutes, adding more unbleached white flour as necessary. Knead until dough is fairly smooth and elastic; it should spring back when indented with fingers.
4. Shape dough into a loaf and butter a loaf pan. Place dough in it, seam side up first, then seam side down. Brush top of loaf with melted butter or safflower oil. Cover and let rise in a warm, draft-free spot until doubled in bulk, about 1½ to 2 hours.
5. Ten to 15 minutes before the end of the rising time preheat oven to 375°F. Bake bread 35 to 40 minutes, or until it sounds hollow when you tap it. Remove from the pan and cool on a rack.

Texas Cornbread

1 cup stoneground cornmeal
½ cup whole wheat flour
½ teaspoon sea salt
1 tablespoon baking powder
½ teaspoon baking soda
1 cup plain yogurt or sour milk or buttermilk
½ cup milk
2 tablespoons mild honey
2 eggs
3 tablespoons butter

1. Preheat oven to 450°F.
2. Sift together cornmeal, whole wheat flour, salt, baking powder, and baking soda in a large bowl. Beat together yogurt, milk, honey, and eggs in another bowl.
3. Place butter in a 9 x 9 inch baking pan and place pan in oven for about 3 minutes, or until butter melts. Remove from heat, brush butter over sides and bottom of pan, and pour remaining melted butter into yogurt and egg mixture. Stir together well and fold into dry mixture. Do this quickly, with just a few strokes of a wooden spoon or plastic spatula. It doesn't matter if there are lumps. The important thing is not to overwork the batter.
4. Pour batter into the warm, greased pan, place in oven, and bake 30 minutes, or until top is beginning to brown and a toothpick inserted comes out clean. Remove from heat and let cool in pan. Eat warm or cool, with honey.

Moist Pumpernickel

Makes 2 loaves

2 tablespoons active dry yeast
½ cup lukewarm water
2 tablespoons safflower oil
2 tablespoons caraway seeds
1 scant tablespoon sea salt
3 tablespoons molasses
2 cups milk, scalded and cooled to lukewarm
2 cups mashed potatoes
1½ cups flaked bran
½ cup wheat germ
2½ cups rye flour
3 cups whole wheat flour
Up to 1 cup unbleached white flour, for kneading
1 egg, beaten with 2 tablespoons water for egg wash
Poppy seeds for topping

1. Dissolve yeast in lukewarm water and allow to stand until it bubbles. Meanwhile, put oil, caraway seeds, salt, and molasses in a large bowl and pour in milk. Make sure milk is lukewarm and stir in yeast mixture. Stir together well.

2. Stir in mashed potatoes, bran, wheat germ and rye flour, a cup at a time, and mix well. Fold in whole wheat flour a cup at a time. The dough should be coming away from the sides of the bowl before you finish adding the whole wheat flour.

3. Place whatever remains of the whole wheat flour on work surface (use unbleached white if none remains). Turn out dough and scrape out what remains in bowl. Flour hands and begin to knead. The dough will be sticky. Knead 10 to 15 minutes, adding unbleached white flour as necessary, but remembering that the dough remains somewhat sticky. When dough is stiff, oil bowl, form dough into a ball, and place in bowl seam side up first, then seam side down. Cover with a towel or plastic wrap and place in a warm spot to rise until doubled in bulk, about 1½ to 2 hours.

4. Punch down dough and turn out onto a lightly floured board. Knead

a few times and divide into 2 pieces, which should weigh about 2½ pounds each. Oil a baking sheet or bread pans and shape into loaves. The dough will be moist. Slash dough with a razor blade or a sharp knife and let rise, covered, 45 to 50 minutes.

5. Toward the end of the rising time preheat oven to 375°F. Place loaves in oven and set timer for 15 minutes. After this time brush with egg wash and sprinkle with poppy seeds. Bake another 30 to 35 minutes, and cool on a rack.

Note: This freezes well.

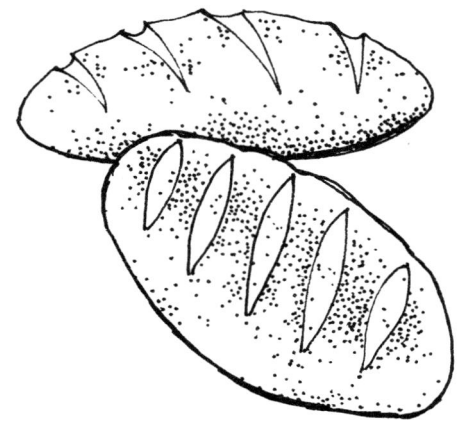

Pain d'Épices

½ cup unsalted butter or safflower oil
⅓ cup strong honey
2 tablespoons molasses
¾ cup milk
1 egg, beaten
1 tablespoon lemon juice
2 cups whole wheat flour
½ cup rye flour
1 teaspoon baking soda
1½ tablespoons anise seeds, ground
¼ teaspoon ground allspice
½ teaspoon ground cardamom
½ teaspoon ground coriander
½ teaspoon grated nutmeg
¼ teaspoon ground cloves
Pinch of sea salt

1. Preheat oven to 375°F.
2. Cream together butter or safflower oil, honey, and molasses. Beat in milk, egg, and lemon juice.
3. Sift together flours, baking soda, and spices. Stir into liquid mixture and blend well.
4. Butter a loaf pan and line with buttered waxed paper. Spoon in batter and bake in preheated oven 50 to 60 minutes, or until a tester comes out clean. Turn out onto a wire rack and remove paper. Cool completely and wrap tightly in plastic and foil. Let sit several days before eating so that spices can ripen. This will stay fresh two weeks.

Herbed Rye and Whole Wheat Bread

Makes 1 loaf

1 tablespoon active dry yeast
1 cup lukewarm water
1 tablespoon mild honey
½ medium onion, minced
3 tablespoons, in all, safflower oil
1½ teaspoons sea salt
½ cup plain yogurt
1 tablespoon dill seed
1 teaspoon dried thyme
1 teaspoon dried sage
2 cups rye flour
3 to 4 cups whole wheat flour

1. Dissolve yeast in water in a large bowl. Add honey and let proof 10 minutes. Meanwhile heat 1 tablespoon safflower oil in a frying pan and sauté onion until tender. Remove from heat and cool.
2. When yeast is bubbly, stir in remaining 2 tablespoons safflower oil, salt, yogurt, herbs, and rye flour. Fold in whole wheat flour, a cup at a time, and when dough can be turned out of bowl place a cup of flour on kneading surface and turn out dough. Knead 10 minutes, adding flour as necessary, until dough is stiff and elastic. Shape into a ball, oil the bowl, and place dough in it rounded side down first, then rounded side up. Cover dough and let rise in a warm spot 1½ hours, or until doubled in bulk.
3. Punch down dough and turn out onto kneading surface. Shape into a loaf and place in an oiled bread pan, seam side down first, then seam side up. Cover with a towel and let rise in a warm spot until surface rises above edges of bread pan, about 45 minutes to an hour. Meanwhile preheat oven to 350°F.
4. Slash dough and bake in preheated oven 50 minutes, or until brown and it responds to tapping with a hollow, thumping sound. Remove from pan, and cool on a rack.

Note: This bread freezes well.

Rye-Oatmeal Bread with Anise and Raisins

Makes 2 loaves

This is a great breakfast bread.

For the sponge:
2 tablespoons active dry yeast
3 cups lukewarm water
3 tablespoons strong or mild honey
3 tablespoons molasses
2 cups unbleached white flour
2 cups whole wheat flour
For the dough:
4 tablespoons safflower oil
2 teaspoons sea salt
2 tablespoons crushed anise seeds
2 tablespoons grated orange rind
2 cups rolled oats
1 cup raisins
2 cups rye flour
1 cup whole wheat flour
Unbleached white flour as necessary
1 egg, beaten, for egg wash

1. Make sponge. In a large bowl dissolve yeast in lukewarm water and add honey and molasses. Stir in unbleached flour and whole wheat flour, a cup at a time. When all the flour has been added, stir about 100 times to incorporate well. Cover with plastic wrap or a damp towel and set in a warm place to rise for an hour. By the end of this time it should be bubbling away.
2. Make dough. Fold in safflower oil and salt, then anise seeds and orange rind, then oatmeal and raisins. Fold in rye flour, a cup at a time, and whole wheat flour. By now you should be able to turn bread out onto kneading surface.
3. Flour kneading surface generously with unbleached white flour and scrape

out dough. Flour hands, and begin to knead. Knead 10 to 15 minutes, adding unbleached white flour as necessary, until dough is stiff and elastic.
4. Shape dough into a ball, oil bowl, and place dough in it seam side up first, then seam side down. Cover and let rise in a warm place 1 hour.
5. Punch down dough and let rise again, covered, 50 minutes.
6. Now turn onto a lightly floured board, knead a few times, and divide into two equal pieces. Form into loaves and place in oiled bread pans, upside down first, then rightside up. Let rise 15 to 25 minutes, or until loaves rise above edges of pans, while you preheat oven to 350°F.
7. Brush loaves with beaten egg, slash with a sharp knife or razor blade, and bake in preheated oven 50 to 55 minutes, until bread is brown on top and responds to tapping with a hollow, thumping noise. Remove from pans and cool on a rack.

Note: This can be frozen.

Rye and Sage Muffins
Makes 12

1 cup whole wheat flour
1 cup rye flour
2 teaspoons baking powder
½ teaspoon sea salt
1 teaspoon sage
2 eggs
¼ cup safflower oil
1 tablespoon mild honey
1 cup plain yogurt
1 tablespoon grated onion

1. Preheat oven to 375°F. Butter muffin tins.
2. Sift together flours, baking powder, salt, and sage.
3. Beat together eggs, safflower oil, yogurt, honey, and grated onion. Quickly stir into dry ingredients. Spoon into prepared muffin tins.
4. Bake 20 minutes in preheated oven. Cool on a rack, or serve warm.

Note: These can be frozen.

Orange Date Muffins
Makes 18

1 cup whole wheat flour
½ cup unbleached white flour
2 teaspoons baking powder
½ teaspoon salt
½ cup wheat germ
2 oranges
½ cup milk
¼ cup melted butter
2 eggs
½ cup mild honey
½ cup chopped dates

1. Preheat oven to 375°F. Butter muffin tins.
2. Squeeze enough juice from oranges to make ½ cup. Combine with milk. Take one of the squeezed oranges and chop coarsely. Place chopped rind in a blender with milk, butter, eggs, and honey and blend until finely chopped.
3. Stir wet mixture into dry ingredients and quickly mix together. Fold in dates. Spoon into prepared muffin tins and bake 20 minutes in preheated oven. Cool on a rack, or eat warm.

Note: These can be frozen.

Zucchini-Carrot Muffins
Makes 24

1½ cups whole wheat flour
½ cup unbleached white flour
4 tablespoons powdered milk
1 tablespoon baking powder
½ teaspoon sea salt
½ teaspoon allspice
½ teaspoon nutmeg
1 teaspoon cinnamon
3 eggs
¼ cup safflower oil
½ cup mild honey
4 heaping tablespoons orange or ginger marmalade
1 teaspoon vanilla
½ cup milk
1 cup grated carrot
1 cup grated zucchini
½ cup chopped walnuts

1. Preheat oven to 375°F. Butter muffin tins.
2. Sift together flours, powdered milk, baking powder, salt, and spices.
3. Beat together eggs, oil, honey, marmalade, vanilla, and milk. Stir in grated carrot and zucchini.
4. Quickly stir wet ingredients into dry, and fold in walnuts. Spoon into muffin tins, filling ¾ full, and bake in preheated oven 20 minutes. Cool on a rack, or serve warm.

Banana Nut Muffins

Makes 16

1 cup whole wheat flour
1 cup unbleached white flour
1 teaspoon baking soda
¾ teaspoon cinnamon
½ teaspoon nutmeg
¼ cup safflower oil
½ cup mild honey
1 teaspoon vanilla
2 eggs
Grated rind of 1 lemon
3 medium bananas, mashed
4 tablespoons plain yogurt
½ cup chopped walnuts

1. Preheat oven to 375°F. Butter muffin tins.
2. Sift together flours, baking soda, and spices.
3. Beat together oil, honey, vanilla, and eggs. Stir in lemon rind, mashed banana, and yogurt. Mix well.
4. Quickly stir wet ingredients into dry, along with walnuts. Spoon into buttered muffin tins and bake 20 minutes in preheated oven. Cool on racks, or serve warm.

Wheat Germ and Fruit Muffins

Makes 15

1 cup unbleached white flour
1 tablespoon baking powder
½ teaspoon sea salt
1 teaspoon ground cinnamon
½ teaspoon allspice
1 cup toasted wheat germ
2 eggs
⅓ cup melted butter
3 tablespoons mild honey
2 tablespoons brandy
1 teaspoon vanilla
1 cup milk
1 cup chopped fresh fruit, such as peaches, apples, pears, or berries

1. Preheat oven to 375°F. Butter muffin tins.
2. Sift together flour, baking powder, salt, spices, and wheat germ.
3. Beat together eggs, butter, honey, brandy, vanilla, and milk. Quickly stir into dry ingredients. Fold in fresh fruit.
4. Spoon into muffin tins and bake 20 minutes in preheated oven. Cool on a rack, or serve warm.

Leftover Grains Muffins
Makes 15

This is a great way to use up last night's cooked grains. The texture will vary depending on what grains you use. Cooked brown rice yields a chewy, hearty muffin; bulghur, couscous, and millet yield a lighter, moister muffin.

½ cup chopped dried apricots or figs
1¼ cups whole wheat flour
2 teaspoons baking powder
½ teaspoon sea salt
2 tablespoons mild honey
¼ cup melted butter
2 eggs
⅔ cup milk
½ teaspoon almond extract
1 cup cooked brown rice, millet, couscous, bulghur, or other grains

1. Preheat oven to 400°F. Butter muffin tins.
2. Place dried apricots or figs in a bowl and cover with boiling water. Let sit 5 to 10 minutes.
3. Sift together flour, baking powder, and sea salt.
4. Beat together eggs, honey, melted butter, milk, and almond extract. Stir in cooked grains.
5. Drain fruit, squeeze out water, and chop.
6. Quickly stir wet ingredients into dry, and fold in chopped, dried fruit. Spoon into muffin tins.
7. Bake 20 minutes in preheated oven. Cool on a rack, or serve warm.

Scones

Makes 24

1 cup yogurt or sour milk or buttermilk
1 egg
3 tablespoons mild honey
3 cups whole wheat pastry flour
2 teaspoons baking powder
1 teaspoon baking soda
½ teaspoon sea salt
⅓ cup melted butter
½ cup currants
1½ tablespoons grated orange peel

1. Preheat oven to 400°F. Butter two baking sheets.
2. Beat together yogurt or milk, egg, and honey in a large bowl. Sift together flour, baking powder, baking soda, and sea salt. Stir ⅔ of flour mixture into milk mixture, a cup at a time, and mix well. Gradually add melted butter, mixing in well. Stir in currants, orange peel, and remaining flour. Mix together with hands or a wooden spoon until dough is stiff enough to knead. Add a little more flour if necessary.
3. Turn out onto a lightly floured board and knead about 10 times, just until ingredients are combined. Divide dough into 4 equal pieces and press out each piece into a thick circle about 5 to 6 inches in diameter. Cut each circle into quarters and place on baking sheets.
4. Bake 15 to 20 minutes, or until just beginning to brown on top. Serve warm with butter, honey, or preserves.

CHAPTER III

SOUPS

Vegetable Stock

2 quarts water
2 onions, quartered
6 cloves garlic, peeled
2 carrots, coarsely sliced
2 leeks, white part only, cleaned and coarsely sliced
2 potatoes, scrubbed, quartered
2 stalks celery, coarsely sliced
1 bouquet garni
12 peppercorns
1 teaspoon sea salt (more to taste)

Place all ingredients in a soup pot and bring to a simmer. Simmer uncovered 1 to 2 hours. Strain and discard vegetables.

Note: This can be frozen and will keep for a few days in the refrigerator. For a stronger, "meatier" broth, add 1 teaspoon *Vegex* and 1 teaspoon soy sauce.

Lentil and Sorrel Soup

Serves 4

1 tablespoon safflower oil
½ onion, chopped
2 cloves garlic, minced
1 cup lentils, washed
1 quart water
1 bay leaf
Sea salt and freshly ground black pepper
¼ pound sorrel, chopped fine
4 tablespoons milk or cream

1. Heat oil in a heavy-bottomed soup pot and add onion and garlic. Sauté until onion is tender and add lentils, water, and bay leaf. Bring to a boil, reduce heat, cover and cook 1 hour, or until lentils are tender. Add salt and freshly ground pepper to taste and remove bay leaf.
2. Purée lentils in a blender or through a food mill. Return to pot and bring to a simmer.
3. Add sorrel and cook 5 to 10 minutes. Correct seasonings, adding more garlic, salt, and pepper if you wish.
4. Stir in milk or cream, and serve.

Sorrel Soup

Serves 3 to 4

1 medium or large potato, peeled and diced
3 cups vegetable stock
1 bunch sorrel, about ¼ lb
Sea salt and freshly ground pepper
1 cup milk
Yogurt or crème fraiche for topping

1. Combine potato and stock and simmer 15 minutes, or until potato is

tender. Add sorrel and cook 5 more minutes.
2. Purée soup in a blender and return to pot. Season to taste with salt and freshly ground pepper, stir in milk, and heat through just to boiling point. Serve, garnishing each bowl with a spoonful of yogurt or crème fraiche.

Hot or Chilled Dill Soup
Serves 6

1½ quarts vegetable stock
2 pounds potatoes, peeled and diced
2 carrots, coarsely sliced
1 onion, coarsely sliced
2 stalks celery, sliced
Sea salt and freshly ground pepper
2 eggs
½ cup chopped, fresh dill
1 cup plain low-fat yogurt

1. Combine vegetable stock, potatoes, carrots, onion, celery, and sea salt in a soup pot or Dutch oven and bring to a boil. Cover, reduce heat, and simmer 1 to 2 hours.
2. Remove from heat, strain, and retain broth. Discard half the vegetables. Purée remaining vegetables in a blender or through a food mill (do not use a food processor). Return to pot with remaining stock and mix together well. Season to taste with freshly ground pepper, and add more salt if you wish.
3. Heat soup through, and meanwhile beat together eggs, dill, and yogurt. Stir some of hot soup into this mixture, then gradually stir mixture into soup. Heat through, but do not boil or eggs will curdle. Serve hot, or cool and chill.

Note: This will keep a couple of days in the refrigerator.

Turkish Borscht

Serves 6

1 tablespoon safflower oil
2 medium onions, chopped
3 cloves garlic, chopped
1 pound raw beets, chopped
2 cups shredded cabbage
2 stalks celery, sliced
2 medium potatoes, diced
1 medium green or red pepper, chopped
2 quarts water or vegetable stock
½ pound tomatoes, chopped
Sea salt and freshly ground black pepper
½ teaspoon dill seeds, crushed
Juice of 1 lemon
3 tablespoons chopped, fresh dill
1 cup plain low-fat yogurt

1. Heat oil in a large heavy-bottomed soup pot and add onion and garlic. Sauté a couple of minutes and then add the other vegetables, dill seeds, salt, and pepper. Cook, stirring another minute, then add water or stock. Bring to a boil, cover, reduce heat, and cook 1 hour.
2. Remove 2 cups from pot and purée in a blender or put through a food mill. Return to soup pot. Stir in dill and lemon juice. Correct seasonings.
3. Serve, topping each bowl with a spoonful of yogurt.

Opposite: Cold Cherry-Lemon Soup (page 74) and Cold Tomato Soup with Basil (page 69).

Black Bean Soup

Serves 6 to 8

1 tablespoon safflower oil
1 onion, chopped
4 cloves garlic, minced
1 stalk celery, with leaves, chopped
1 pound black beans, washed and soaked for several hours
6 cups water or vegetable stock
1 bay leaf
1 teaspoon summer savory
Pinch of thyme
Pinch of sage
½ teaspoon celery seed
Sea salt and freshly ground pepper
Juice of 1 lemon
2 tablespoons dry sherry
Croutons and lemon slices for garnish
Chopped, fresh parsley for garnish
Yogurt or crème fraiche for garnish

1. Heat safflower oil in a soup pot or Dutch oven and sauté onion with 2 cloves of garlic and the celery until onion is tender.

2. Drain beans and add to pot, along with water or stock, bay leaf, summer savory, thyme, sage, and celery seed. Bring to a boil, reduce heat, and simmer 1 hour. Add remaining garlic and sea salt and simmer another hour, covered.

3. Remove bay leaf. Purée half the soup in a blender or through a food mill and return to pot. Correct seasoning and add freshly ground pepper to taste. Stir in lemon juice and sherry, heat through, and serve, garnishing with yogurt or crème fraiche, croutons, lemon slices, and parsley.

Note: This can be frozen, and will keep a few days in the refrigerator.

Hot Yogurt Soup with Coriander

This might look strange to you at first glance, but it is an exquisite soup that comes from the Middle East.

½ cup barley, washed
2 cups water
Pinch of sea salt
1 tablespoon safflower oil or butter
1 medium onion, finely chopped
1 clove garlic, put through a press
5 tablespoons chopped, fresh coriander
2½ cups plain yogurt
1 egg, beaten
1 tablespoon cornstarch
3 cups vegetable stock
Salt and freshly ground pepper

1. Combine barley and water in a saucepan, bring to a boil, add a pinch or two of salt, reduce heat, cover, and simmer 45 minutes, or until barley is tender and water evaporated. Set aside.
2. Sauté onion in safflower oil or butter until it begins to brown. Add garlic and continue sautéing until onion is browned, then stir in coriander, sauté about a half minute, and remove from heat.
3. Gently heat yogurt in a heavy-bottomed soup pot and carefully stir in beaten egg. Stir together cornstarch and a couple of tablespoons of water or vegetable stock, and when cornstarch is completely dissolved, stir into yogurt and egg mixture.
4. Add vegetable stock to yogurt and slowly bring to a boil. As soon as it reaches the boiling point, reduce heat to very low, and stir in onion, garlic and coriander, and barley. Add salt and lots of freshly ground pepper, stir together well, and serve.

Potato Soup with Chervil
Serves 6

This soup is fairly thin, and very light and delicate.

1 tablespoon butter (more as needed)
1 onion, chopped
1 clove garlic, chopped
1 pound boiling potatoes, peeled
Pinch of nutmeg
1 quart water
Sea salt and freshly ground black pepper
1 cup milk
2 heaping tablespoons snipped chervil
2-3 tablespoons cream (optional)

1. Heat butter in a soup pot and sauté onion and garlic about 1 minute. Add potatoes and continue to sauté over very low heat 10 minutes, stirring often so that potatoes don't stick or burn. They should not brown.
2. Add a little nutmeg, the water, and some sea salt. Bring to a boil, reduce heat, cover, and simmer 20 to 25 minutes, or until potatoes are quite soft.
3. Purée through a food mill, twice.
4. Heat soup through, and meanwhile bring milk to a boil in another saucepan. Add hot milk to soup, stir in chervil, and add salt and pepper to taste. Add another pinch of nutmeg if you wish. If you want a thicker soup, stir in optional cream. Serve hot.

Rye Caraway Soup

Serves 6 to 8

1 tablespoon safflower oil
1 onion, chopped
1 clove garlic, minced or pressed
1 carrot, minced
1 potato, diced
1 stalk celery, minced
1 cup whole rye
2 teaspoons caraway seeds
½ cup beer
6 cups vegetable stock
Sea salt and freshly ground black pepper
1 cup plain yogurt
2 tablespoons chopped, fresh parsley

1. Heat safflower oil in a soup pot or Dutch oven and sauté onion, garlic, carrot, celery, and potato until onion is translucent. Add rye and caraway seeds, and sauté 2 minutes, stirring.
2. Pour in beer and cook, stirring, until beer is absorbed. Pour in stock, bring to a boil and cover, reduce heat, and simmer 1½ to 2 hours.
3. Purée half the soup in a blender until very smooth. Whisk back into soup. Add sea salt and pepper to taste, and stir in yogurt.
4. Serve, garnishing each bowl with fresh parsley or dill (you need the bright green herbs here for color).

Note: This can be frozen or will keep a few days in the refrigerator.

Cold Tomato Soup with Basil

Serves 4 to 6

1 tablespoon butter or olive oil
3 shallots, chopped
4 cloves garlic, chopped
2 pounds tomatoes, chopped
3 cups water or vegetable stock
Sea salt to taste
2 teaspoons honey
8 leaves fresh basil
1 large handful pearl barley or tapioca
6-8 tablespoons cream or plain yogurt
Juice of ½-1 lemon
2 additional tablespoons fresh basil
2 sprigs fresh mint
Crème fraiche or yogurt for garnish

1. Heat butter or oil in a large, heavy-bottomed soup pot and add shallots and half the garlic. Sauté until shallots are tender, about 2 minutes, and add tomatoes and remaining garlic. Simmer over a medium flame 10 minutes.
2. Add water or stock, salt, honey and 8 leaves of fresh basil, bring to a boil, reduce heat, cover, and simmer 15 minutes.
3. Add tapioca or pearl barley and cook another 15 minutes, or until grains are tender.
4. Remove from heat and purée through the fine blade of a food mill. Stir in cream or yogurt, adjust salt, and refrigerate until thoroughly chilled.
5. Stir in lemon juice to taste and add more garlic if you wish. Slice remaining basil into thin slivers and serve, topping each bowl with an optional spoonful of crème fraiche or yogurt, a sprinkling of basil, and a few leaves of fresh mint.

Note: This can be made a day or two in advance and kept in the refrigerator. It can also be frozen.

Illustrated opposite page 64.

Puréed Pumpkin Soup

Serves 4

1 tablespoon butter or safflower oil
1 small onion, chopped
1 medium clove garlic, minced or pressed
2½ pounds pumpkin, peeled and diced
1 teaspoon paprika
4½ cups water or vegetable stock
Sea salt and freshly ground black pepper to taste
1 teaspoon thyme
4 tablespoons crème fraiche or yogurt, for garnish

1. Heat butter or oil in a large, heavy-bottomed saucepan or soup pot and sauté onion and garlic until onion begins to be tender. Add pumpkin and paprika and sauté another 2 to 3 minutes. Add water or stock and some sea salt (about ½ teaspoon) and bring to a simmer. Cover and simmer 30 minutes.
2. Purée soup through a mouli food mill or in a blender. Return to pot and add thyme, pepper, and more sea salt to taste. Heat through, adjust seasonings, and serve, garnishing each bowl with a spoonful of yogurt or crème fraiche.

SOUPS

Curried Pumpkin Soup
Serves 6 to 8

2 pounds fresh pumpkin, peeled and diced
1 quart milk
4 tablespoons mild honey (more to taste)
2 tablespoons butter
½ teaspoon freshly grated nutmeg (or to taste)
½ teaspoon ground cinnamon
½ teaspoon ground mace
½-1 teaspoon curry powder
¼ teaspoon ground ginger
Sea salt to taste
½ to 1 cup orange juice
1-2 tablespoons orange rind
Whipped cream or plain yogurt for garnish
2 tablespoons sunflower seeds or chopped pecans

1. Steam chopped pumpkin 15 to 20 minutes, or until soft. Purée through a food mill.
2. Combine pumpkin, milk, honey, and butter in a heavy-bottomed saucepan or soup pot and bring to a simmer over low heat. Stir together well to blend. Add spices and salt, and simmer gently 15 minutes. Do not boil.
3. Slowly add orange juice and rind. Simmer, stirring often, another 10 minutes. Correct seasonings and serve, topping each bowl with whipped cream or yogurt and a sprinkling of chopped pecans or sunflower seeds.

Tarragon Soup

Serves 4 to 6

---

6 cups water

3 leeks, white part only, cleaned and cut in large pieces

2 carrots, coarsely sliced

1 stalk celery, coarsely sliced

1 onion, quartered

3 small potatoes, scrubbed and quartered

4 cloves garlic, peeled

1 bay leaf

6 whole peppercorns

Sea salt to taste

Freshly ground black pepper to taste

2 tablespoons chopped, fresh tarragon

3 tablespoons freshly grated Parmesan

2 eggs, beaten (optional)

1. Combine all the ingredients except tarragon, freshly ground pepper, Parmesan, and eggs in a large soup pot and bring to a boil. Reduce heat and simmer uncovered 30 minutes to an hour. Taste and adjust salt. Drain and discard vegetables. Return broth to soup pot.
2. Heat broth and add tarragon and Parmesan. Stir and add freshly ground pepper to taste. Serve at once.
3. For a richer soup, beat eggs in a bowl and spoon in some of the hot soup, to which you have added the tarragon and cheese. Pour this back into the soup pot, heat through but do not boil, and serve.

Sweet Potato Soup
Serves 6

This soup is refreshing served cold, and warming and comforting hot. Garnish it with apple slices for a sweet, crunchy contrast. It will keep up to two days in the refrigerator.

1 tablespoon butter
6 spring onions, white part only, sliced
1 large carrot, diced
1 stalk celery, diced
½ pound tart apples, cored and diced
2 pounds sweet potatoes, peeled and diced
5 cups water or vegetable stock
2 tablespoons mild honey
½ teaspoon cinnamon
¼ teaspoon ground cloves
Juice of 1 large lime
1 cup plain low-fat yogurt
Freshly grated nutmeg to taste
Sea salt to taste
1 additional apple, sliced thin or minced, for garnish
Additional yogurt and sunflower seeds for garnish

1. Heat butter in a heavy-bottomed soup pot and sauté onions, carrot, and celery until onion is tender. Add apples, sweet potatoes, stock, honey, cinnamon, and cloves and bring to a simmer. Cover and reduce heat; simmer 40 minutes.

2. Remove soup from heat and purée in a blender. Return to pot and whisk in lime juice, yogurt, nutmeg, and salt. Heat through, adjust seasonings, and serve, garnishing with chopped apples, yogurt, and sunflower seeds.

Chilled Melon Soup

4 cups ripe cantaloupe, finely chopped
4 cups ripe honeydew, finely chopped
1 cup fresh orange juice, strained
Juice of 2 limes
3 tablespoons mild honey
1 cup chilled champagne
½ cup heavy cream, whipped
Sliced strawberries and fresh mint for garnish

1. Reserve and chill ½ cup each chopped cantaloupe and honeydew. Purée remaining melon with orange juice, lime juice, and honey. Stir in reserved chopped melon. Refrigerate several hours. Just before serving, pour in champagne.
2. Serve in chilled bowls, garnished with mint, whipped cream, and strawberries.

Cold Cherry-Lemon Soup

Serves 6

2½ pounds sweet dark cherries, stemmed, washed, pitted
Juice and grated rind of 2 lemons
5 cups water
4-5 tablespoons mild honey
½ cup semi-dry white wine
1 tablespoon Kirsch
1 cup plain yogurt

1. Set aside 24 cherries. Combine remaining cherries with lemon juice and rind, water, honey, and white wine in a saucepan and bring to a simmer. Simmer 15 to 20 minutes.
2. Drain cherries and retain liquid. Purée in a blender, using some of the liquid to moisten, or through a food mill. Return puréed cherries and their liquid to the pot, stir in Kirsch, and adjust lemon juice and honey.

3. Chill soup several hours. Just before serving stir in yogurt. Serve, garnishing each bowl with 4 of the cherries you set aside.

Illustrated opposite page 64.

Peach-Yogurt Soup
Serves 6

3 pounds ripe peaches
4 tablespoons mild honey
3 tablespoons lemon juice
5 cups plain yogurt
1 cup fresh orange juice
3 tablespoons peach brandy (optional)
½ teaspoon cinnamon
½ teaspoon freshly grated nutmeg
¼ teaspoon ground ginger
½ teaspoon ground cardamom
½ teaspoon vanilla
½ cup slivered almonds for garnish

1. Set aside 6 of the peaches. Remove pits from remaining peaches and purée in a blender or through a food mill, along with honey and lemon juice. Place in a large bowl and stir in yogurt, optional brandy, orange juice, spices, and vanilla. Slice peaches you set aside and add to soup.
2. Serve, or cover and chill before serving. Garnish each bowl with slivered almonds.

Fruit Soup

Serves 6 to 8

Perfect for a summer lunch or dinner, this is good hot or chilled.

1 pound peaches, peeled,* sliced
1 pound plums, sliced
1 pound nectarines, sliced
½ pound tart apples, peeled, cored, sliced
1 banana, peeled and sliced
1 quart water
Juice of 1 lemon
3 tablespoons mild honey
2 tablespoons tapioca
6-8 tablespoons plain low-fat yogurt

1. Combine fruit and water and bring to a boil. Reduce heat, cover, and cook 15 minutes. Add lemon juice, honey, and tapioca and continue to cook until mixture thickens.

2. Remove soup from heat. Serve either hot or chilled, topping each bowl with a tablespoon of yogurt.

* To peel peaches, blanch in boiling water, run under cold water, and gently peel off skin.

Chilled Cranberry Soup with Pomegranate Seeds

Serves 4 to 6

¾ pound cranberries
1 small onion, chopped
5 cups vegetable stock or water
1-2 teaspoons curry powder
½ cup orange juice
¼ cup mild honey
1 tablespoon cornstarch
½ cup plain low-fat yogurt
½ cup cream
1-2 tablespoons lemon juice (more to taste)
¼ to ½ cup red wine, to taste
Additional yogurt for garnish (optional)
½ orange, cut in thin slices
½ cup pomegranate seeds

1. Combine cranberries, onion, vegetable stock, and curry powder and bring to a boil. Reduce heat, cover, and simmer 10 minutes.
2. Dissolve cornstarch in orange juice and add to soup, along with honey. Simmer another 10 minutes. Remove from heat, let cool a moment, and purée in a blender with yogurt. Strain and stir in cream, lemon juice, and wine.
3. Cover and chill several hours or overnight. The flavor will mature during this time, so don't be concerned if it tastes rather flat before you chill it.
4. Serve chilled soup, topping each bowl with a spoonful of yogurt, a slice of orange, and a spoonful of pomegranate seeds.

CHAPTER IV

VEGETABLES, LEGUMES, GRAINS, TOFU, AND PASTA

Potatoes with Pesto

Serves 4 to 6

No book on herb cookery would be complete without this marvelous thick basil sauce. It is not only terrific with pasta but also as a sauce for potatoes, a dressing for a tomato salad, or a filling for mushrooms (see recipes).

2 cups fresh basil leaves
3 tablespoons pine nuts
2 large cloves garlic
Sea salt to taste
½ cup virgin olive oil
½ cup freshly grated Parmesan cheese
2 tablespoons freshly grated Romano cheese
2 pounds new or boiling potatoes
2 teaspoons butter (optional)

1. Place basil, pine nuts, garlic, and salt in a food processor fitted with the steel blade or in a blender. Turn on and pour in olive oil. Process until you have a fairly smooth paste. If you are using a blender you will have to stop and start it to stir down the mixture.

2. Remove from food processor or blender and stir in cheeses. Adjust salt, and set aside.
3. Cut potatoes into quarters and steam until tender. Drain and toss with pesto. If you wish, add a teaspoon or two of butter. Serve at once.

Mushrooms Stuffed with Pesto

Serves 4

1 batch Pesto (page 78)
16 very large or 20-24 smaller mushrooms
2 tablespoons olive oil
Sea salt and freshly ground black pepper

1. Preheat oven to 400°F.
2. Make pesto.
3. Clean mushrooms. Twist off stems and set aside for another use. Salt and pepper the inside of the mushroom caps.
4. Oil a baking dish with some of the olive oil. Place mushroom caps on it rounded side down, and fill open side of caps with pesto. Drizzle on the rest of the olive oil and place in preheated oven.
5. Bake 15 to 20 minutes, basting occasionally with juices the mushrooms release. The mushrooms should be cooked through and the pesto just beginning to brown on the top.

Note: The mushrooms can be cleaned, filled, and kept in the refrigerator for several hours.

Spiral Pasta with Rich Tomato Sauce

Serves 4 to 6

1 tablespoon olive oil
1 onion, chopped
4 cloves garlic, minced
2 pounds ripe tomatoes, chopped
½ cup tomato paste
1 bay leaf
2 teaspoons oregano
1 tablespoon chopped, fresh basil, or 1 teaspoon dried
Pinch of cinnamon
Sea salt and freshly ground black pepper
½ pound spiral-shaped pasta
1 cup freshly grated Parmesan

1. Heat olive oil in a heavy-bottomed saucepan and add onion and 2 cloves of the garlic. Sauté until onion is tender and add tomatoes, tomato paste, and bay leaf. Bring to a simmer, cover, and simmer 30 minutes.
2. Add remaining garlic, oregano, basil, cinnamon and salt to tomato sauce. Continue to simmer, uncovered, another 30 minutes or even longer. Adjust seasonings and add freshly ground pepper to taste. If the sauce tastes a little bitter, add a teaspoon of honey.
3. Bring a large pot of water to a boil, add salt and a spoonful of cooking oil, and pasta. Cook until *al dente*, drain, and toss immediately with tomato sauce in a warm casserole. Serve at once with fresh grated Parmesan on the side.

Note: The sauce freezes well and will keep several days in the refrigerator.

Illustrated opposite.

Opposite: Spiral Pasta in Rich Tomato Sauce (above) and Sweet and Sour Red Peppers (page 96).

Greek Style White Beans
Serves 6 to 8

> 1 pound white beans, washed and soaked
> 1 tablespoon olive oil
> 1 onion, chopped
> 8 cloves garlic, peeled and crushed
> 5 cups water
> 1 bay leaf
> 1 teaspoon oregano
> 2 tablespoons tomato paste
> Sea salt and freshly ground black pepper
> Juice of 1 large lemon (more to taste)
> ½ cup chopped, fresh parsley
> ½ red onion, minced
> Additional garlic (optional)
> Greek olives for garnish

1. Heat the tablespoon of olive oil in a large bean pot or soup pot and sauté onion until it begins to soften. Add garlic and sauté a few minutes longer.
2. Drain beans and add to the pot, along with water, bay leaf, oregano, and tomato paste. Bring to a boil, cover, reduce heat, and simmer 1 to 2 hours, or until beans are tender. Season to taste with sea salt and freshly ground pepper.
3. Remove beans from heat and add lemon juice, parsley, and chopped red onion. Add more garlic if you wish. Serve garnished with Greek black olives.
4. This can also be served cold. In that case, do not add lemon juice, parsley, and onion right away. Chill and add shortly before serving. Add more garlic if you wish, and garnish with olives.

Red Bean Goulash

Serves 6 to 8

1 tablespoon safflower oil
2 onions, chopped
4 large cloves garlic, minced
2 carrots, sliced
2 stalks celery, chopped, with leaves
1 pound red beans, washed and soaked overnight
1 teaspoon summer savory
1 teaspoon oregano
1½ pounds tomatoes, peeled, chopped (may use canned)
2 quarts water
1 bay leaf
Sea salt and freshly ground black pepper
2 additional tablespoons safflower oil
1 additional small onion, minced
2-3 additional cloves garlic, minced
2 tablespoons unbleached white flour
2 tablespoons paprika
The liquid from the beans
½ cup minced parsley
2 tablespoons wine vinegar
Additional sea salt, pepper, and paprika to taste
Yogurt or crème fraiche and chives for garnish
½ pound wide whole wheat noodles (optional)

1. Heat 1 tablespoon safflower oil in a large bean pot or soup pot and sauté onions with 2 cloves of garlic until onions begin to soften. Add carrots and celery and continue to sauté a few more minutes. Drain beans, rinse, and add to the pot, along with summer savory, oregano, tomatoes, water, and bay leaf. Bring to a boil, cover, and reduce heat. Simmer 2 hours, adding remaining 2 cloves of garlic and salt to taste halfway through the cooking.

2. Correct seasoning for beans, adding freshly ground pepper to taste, and more sea salt and garlic if you wish. Drain and retain liquid.

3. In a heavy-bottomed saucepan or frying pan, heat the additional 2 tablespoons of safflower oil and add additional onion and 2 cloves of garlic. Sauté over low heat until onion is soft. Add unbleached white flour and paprika and stir together with a wooden spoon. Cook this roux over low heat about 3 minutes, stirring.
4. Off the heat, whisk liquid from beans into roux. Return to heat and bring to a simmer, stirring. When mixture is thick, stir back into beans. Add parsley and vinegar, bring to a simmer, taste, and adjust seasonings.
5. Serve, topping, if you like, with yogurt or crème fraiche and chives.

Note: This makes a complete, filling meal if served with whole wheat noodles. Try to find wide ones, which will give the dish a more Hungarian nature. This can be frozen and will keep about 3 days in the refrigerator.

Carrots with Caraway Seeds

Serves 4

1 pound carrots, sliced thin
1 tablespoon safflower oil
1 large clove garlic, minced or pressed
1 teaspoon crushed caraway seeds
Sea salt and freshly ground black pepper
1 cup plain yogurt

1. Steam carrots 5 to 10 minutes, or until crisp-tender. Refresh under cold water.
2. Heat safflower oil in a frying pan and add garlic. Sauté a minute or two and add carrots and caraway seeds. Stir-fry about 1 or 2 minutes, add salt and pepper to taste, and remove from heat. Transfer to a serving bowl, stir in yogurt, toss well, and serve.

Spicy Eggplant Purée

Serves 4

1 pound eggplant
Olive oil
1-2 cloves garlic, minced or pressed, to taste
½ cup plain low-fat yogurt
2 tablespoons chopped, fresh mint
1 tablespoon chopped chives
Sea salt and freshly ground black pepper
1 tomato, chopped
Juice of ½-1 lemon
Cayenne to taste
Strips of green or red pepper

1. Preheat oven to 450°F. Cut eggplant in half lengthwise and score with a

sharp knife down the middle, to the skin but not through it. Oil a baking sheet with olive oil and place the eggplant on it, cut side down. Bake in the hot oven 15 to 20 minutes, or until thoroughly soft and the skin is shrivelled. Remove from oven and allow to cool.
2. Scoop eggplant out from skin and mash in a mortar and pestle or in a food processor. Blend in remaining ingredients, except strips of pepper. Transfer to a bowl and chill.
3. Serve with strips of red or green pepper as dippers.

Black or Pinto Beans with Coriander

Fresh coriander is a typically Mexican addition to beans, and ever since my first taste of beans seasoned with this herb, years ago in a Mexican border town, black beans and pintos just don't taste complete to me without it.

1 pound black or pinto beans, washed, picked over, and soaked overnight
1 tablespoon safflower oil
1 large onion, minced
4 large cloves garlic, minced or pressed
6 cups water
Sea salt to taste
3-4 tablespoons chopped, fresh coriander

1. Soak beans overnight or for several hours and drain.
2. Heat safflower oil in a large, heavy-bottomed soup pot or casserole and sauté onion with half the garlic until onion is tender. Add beans and water and bring to a boil. Reduce heat, cover, and simmer 1 hour.
3. Add remaining garlic and coriander. Add salt to taste and continue to cook another hour, or until beans are tender and broth thick and savory. You may wish to add more garlic or salt.
4. Serve with rice, tortillas, cornbread, or other whole grain bread.

Note: These can be frozen and will keep up to 3 days in the refrigerator.

Rice with Tofu, Potatoes, and Cumin

Serves 6

3 cups water (more as needed)
2 tablespoons safflower oil (more as needed)
2 teaspoons whole cumin seeds
1 large or 2 small potatoes, scrubbed and diced small
4 ounces tofu, diced
1½ cups raw brown rice
¼-½ teaspoon sea salt, to taste
½ teaspoon turmeric

1. Have water simmering.
2. Heat oil in a heavy-bottomed saucepan and add cumin seeds. When they begin to pop, after about 15 seconds, add potatoes and tofu. Cook, stirring, until potatoes begin to brown. Add rice and a little more oil if pan is too dry, and cook, stirring, a couple of minutes.
3. Add water, salt, and turmeric, and bring to a boil. Reduce heat, cover, and simmer 35 minutes. Uncover, check liquid, and add a little more if pan is dry. Cook another 5 to 10 minutes, or until liquid is absorbed and rice is cooked through.

Chickpea and Cumin Dip

½ pound chick peas, washed, soaked overnight
2 teaspoons cumin seeds
1 quart water
Sea salt
1 tablespoon olive oil
2 tablespoons plain low-fat yogurt
Juice of 1-2 lemons, to taste
1-2 cloves garlic, to taste
Cooking liquid from the chickpeas
Chopped, fresh mint for garnish

1. Soak chickpeas overnight and drain. Combine with cumin and water in a saucepan and bring to a boil. Reduce heat, cover, and simmer 1 to 2 hours, or until very tender. Add sea salt to taste.
2. Drain chickpeas and retain liquid. Blend with remaining ingredients, except mint, in a blender or food processor, until very smooth. Thin out to desired consistency with cooking liquid. Be sure that you blend up all the cooked cumin seeds with the chickpeas.
3. Adjust seasonings, adding garlic, lemon juice, and salt to taste, and transfer to a bowl. Sprinkle with mint and refrigerate. Serve as a dip with raw vegetables or as a spread.

Note: This will keep a few days in the refrigerator.

Kasha with Mushrooms and Dill

Serves 4 generously

2½ cups vegetable stock
1 cup buckwheat groats
1 egg, beaten
1 tablespoon safflower oil or butter (more as needed)
1 small onion, chopped
½ pound mushrooms, cleaned and sliced
Sea salt and freshly ground black pepper
1 tablespoon brandy (optional)
2 tablespoons chopped, fresh dill
Soy sauce to taste (optional)
Plain yogurt for topping

1. Have stock simmering in a saucepan.
2. Mix together buckwheat groats and egg in a bowl. Heat a dry saucepan over a medium flame and add groats. Cook, stirring over dry heat, until all the egg is absorbed and grains are separate.
3. Add stock to groats. When it boils, cover, reduce heat, and cook 20 to 30 minutes, or until liquid is absorbed. Remove from heat.
4. Heat 1 tablespoon safflower oil or butter in a frying pan and add chopped onion. Sauté until onion is tender and add mushrooms. Cook, stirring, until they begin to soften and add salt, pepper, and brandy. Cook a minute, then add more butter or oil if necessary and stir in kasha and dill. Toss together until heated through, add soy sauce if you wish, and serve, topping with plain yogurt if desired.

New Potatoes with Dill

Serves 4 to 6

2 pounds small new potatoes
1 tablespoon butter

1-2 tablespoons chopped, fresh dill
Sea salt and freshly ground black pepper

1. Scrub potatoes and steam until tender, about 15 to 20 minutes.
2. Heat butter in a frying pan or casserole, add potatoes, toss until coated with butter, and add dill. Add salt and pepper to taste, toss together, and serve.

Tofu and Broccoli with Fennel

Serves 6

1 bunch broccoli (about 2 pounds)
1 tablespoon safflower or vegetable oil
1 clove garlic, minced or pressed
1 teaspoon grated, fresh ginger, or ¼ teaspoon ground
2 spring onions
½ pound tofu, diced
2 tablespoons soy sauce, preferably tamari
1 tomato, diced
1 tablespoon dry sherry (optional)
1-2 tablespoons chopped fresh fennel
1 tablespoon cornstarch dissolved in 2 tablespoons water

1. Break broccoli into florets, peel and slice stems, and steam 10 minutes. Refresh under cold water and set aside.
2. Heat safflower oil in a wide frying pan or wok and add garlic and ginger. Sauté a few seconds and add sliced spring onions and tofu. Cook, stirring over medium-high heat about 2 minutes, then add soy sauce and tomato. Stir-fry 3 to 5 minutes, and add broccoli and sherry. Continue to stir-fry another 3 minutes.
3. Add fennel, stir well, then stir in dissolved cornstarch. Cook, stirring, until vegetables are glazed.
4. Remove from heat and serve at once over hot cooked grains. Pass round additional soy sauce.

Pasta e Fagiole

Serves 6 to 8

1 pound white beans
2 quarts water
2 large onions, chopped
8 cloves garlic, minced or pressed
2 tablespoons olive or vegetable oil
2 pounds tomatoes, quartered
3 tablespoons tomato paste
2 sprigs parsley
1 bay leaf
1 small dried, red pepper
1 teaspoon marjoram or oregano
1 tablespoon chopped, fresh basil, or 1 teaspoon dried
½ teaspoon thyme
½ teaspoon rosemary
Sea salt and freshly ground black pepper to taste
¾ pound pasta, either small macaroni, spirals, or fettucine
1½ cups freshly grated Parmesan
4 tablespoons chopped, fresh parsley

1. Wash beans, pick over, and soak overnight or for several hours in the water.
2. Heat olive or vegetable oil in a large, heavy-bottomed soup pot and sauté onions and 3 cloves of garlic until onions are tender. Add beans and their liquid, tomatoes and tomato paste, and bring to a boil. Add 3 more cloves of the garlic, the 2 sprigs of parsley and the bay leaf, cover, reduce heat, and simmer 1 hour. Add dried pepper and simmer another hour. Remove red pepper, bay leaf and parsley, and add remaining garlic, sea salt and freshly ground pepper to taste, marjoram or oregano, basil, thyme, and rosemary. Simmer 15 minutes. Remove 2 cups of the beans and enough broth to moisten, and purée in a blender. Return to pot and adjust seasonings. Add pasta and simmer until cooked. Stir in half the Parmesan and the parsley, stir to melt through, and serve. Pass round remaining cheese and also a pepper mill.

Note: The dish can be made, up to the addition of the pasta, a day or two in advance, and before adding the pasta it can be frozen. When served it should be quite thick and soupy.

Zucchini Gratin
Serves 4 to 6

3 pounds zucchini
2 tablespoons unsalted butter
1 tablespoon milk
Sea salt and freshly ground black pepper
2 tablespoons chopped, fresh marjoram
3 tablespoons chopped, fresh parsley
¾ cup grated Gruyère cheese
Additional butter (optional)

1. Preheat oven to 400°F.
2. Cut zucchini in half and scoop out seeds. Chop and steam 10 minutes, or until soft.
3. Remove from heat and mash with the back of a spoon or purée through a food mill. Add butter and milk and salt and pepper to taste. Stir in marjoram and parsley.
4. Butter a shallow baking or gratin dish and spread zucchini evenly over the bottom. Sprinkle with cheese, and if you wish, dot with a little butter.
5. Bake in the preheated oven 15 minutes, or until cheese is lightly browned.

Lentils and Bulghur with Parsley and Mint

Serves 4

2 tablespoons olive oil
1 onion, chopped
3 cloves garlic, minced
⅔ cup lentils, washed
2½ cups water
1 bay leaf
Sea salt and freshly ground black pepper to taste
⅔ cup bulghur
1 teaspoon ground cumin
1 teaspoon ground coriander seeds
3 tablespoons chopped, fresh parsley
2 tablespoons chopped, fresh mint
Plain yogurt for topping (optional)

1. Heat 1 tablespoon of olive oil in a heavy-bottomed saucepan or Dutch oven and add half the onion and 2 cloves of garlic. Sauté 2 minutes, or until onion is soft.
2. Stir in lentils, water, and bay leaf and bring to a boil. Add salt, reduce heat, cover, and simmer 30 to 45 minutes, or until lentils are soft but not mushy. Adjust seasonings, add some pepper, and remove bay leaf.
3. Stir in bulghur, cover pot, and let sit 30 minutes to an hour off the heat. Stir once to make sure all the bulghur is being infused with the cooking liquid.
4. Heat remaining tablespoon of olive oil in a wide frying pan and add remaining onion and garlic. Sauté a minute or two and stir in cumin and coriander. Sauté another couple of minutes and stir in lentils and bulghur. Cook, stirring, a minute or two to heat through, and stir in parsley and mint. Adjust seasonings and serve. Top with plain yogurt if you like.

Note: This will keep up to three days in the refrigerator, and it makes a good stuffing for vegetables (see following recipe).

Tomatoes and Zucchini Stuffed with Lentils and Bulghur

Serves 4 to 6

1 recipe Lentils and Bulghur with Parsley and Mint (page 92)
4-6 firm, ripe tomatoes
4-6 small zucchini
Plain low-fat yogurt for garnish
Additional parsley and mint for garnish

1. Cook lentils and bulghur as in the recipe on page 92, up to Step 4.
2. Preheat oven to 350°F.
3. Cut tops off tomatoes, about ½ inch down from stems, and scoop out seeds with a small spoon. Discard seeds and gently scoop or cut out some of the inner flesh. Chop flesh.
4. Cut zucchini in half lengthwise and steam 5 minutes in a covered pot. Remove from heat, refresh under cold water, and pat dry. Using a small spoon, carefully scoop out seeds and some of the inner flesh, leaving a ½ inch thick shell. Chop scooped out zucchini.
5. Now proceed with Step 4 of the Lentils and Bulghur recipe, but add diced tomato and zucchini pulp to the onions. When onion is tender, proceed as directed.
6. Carefully fill tomatoes and zucchini with lentil-bulghur mixture and place in an oiled baking dish. Heat through for 15 minutes in preheated oven and serve, topping if you wish with plain yogurt and chopped fresh parsley and/or mint.

Note: This can be prepared a few hours in advance, up to the baking point.

Parsley Purée
Serves 6

1 pound parsley
2 pound potatoes, peeled
2½ cups milk
2 ounces butter
Sea salt and freshly ground black pepper

1. Cut stems off parsley and quarter potatoes. Place both in a steamer and steam above boiling water 20 minutes, or until potatoes are thoroughly soft.
2. Remove from heat and purée through a mouli food mill. Transfer to a bowl.
3. Heat milk to boiling point and stir into potatoes and parsley. Stir in butter, add sea salt and pepper to taste, and beat well to make a smooth, light purée. Serve hot, or chill and serve cold.

Broiled Mushroom Caps
Serves 4

1 pound mushrooms
2 tablespoons olive oil
3 cloves garlic, sliced
½ teaspoon chopped, fresh or crushed, dried rosemary
¼ teaspoon thyme
Sea salt and freshly ground black pepper

1. Preheat the boiler.
2. Clean mushrooms with a damp cloth, or if very sandy run briefly under cold water and wipe dry. Twist off stems and put aside for another use. Place caps on an oiled baking sheet, rounded side down.
3. Drizzle olive oil over mushrooms and sprinkle with garlic, rosemary,

thyme, and salt and pepper. Place under broiler and cook 10 to 15 minutes, basting every 5 minutes, or until tender and juicy. Remove from heat and serve as a side dish.

Spicy Lentils
Serves 4 to 6

1 tablespoon safflower oil
1 onion, chopped
3 cloves garlic, minced
2 cups lentils, washed
6 cups water
1 bay leaf
1 small, whole cayenne pepper
1 tablespoon tomato paste
Sea salt and freshly ground black pepper
½ teaspoon thyme
Fresh, chopped parsley for garnish

1. Heat oil in a heavy-bottomed soup pot or Dutch oven and add onion and 2 cloves of garlic. Sauté until onion is tender, and add remaining ingredients, except chopped parsley.
2. Bring to a boil, reduce heat, cover, and cook 40 minutes. Remove cayenne pepper and continue to cook until lentils are tender, another 30 minutes or so. Correct seasonings, adding more garlic or sea salt and freshly ground pepper if you wish. Serve garnished with fresh, chopped parsley.

Note: This can be frozen and will keep for a few days in the refrigerator.

Sweet and Sour Red Peppers

Serves 6

2 pounds red peppers
2 onions, sliced
4 large cloves garlic, peeled
2 bay leaves
3 cups water
1 cup good quality vinegar (such as sherry or champagne)
½ teaspoon whole peppercorns
6 tablespoons mild honey
2 sprigs fresh thyme

1. Cut peppers in half lengthwise and remove seeds and membranes. Cut halves in half again, or into thirds if they are very big. You should have very wide strips.

2. Combine remaining ingredients in a casserole and bring to a boil. Add peppers and continue to boil over a fairly high flame for 15 minutes. Remove from heat, let cool, cover, and refrigerate several hours. Serve cold.

Illustrated opposite page 80.

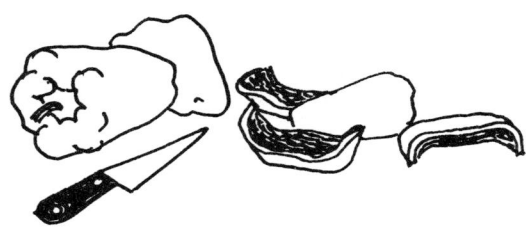

Sweet and Sour Leeks
Serves 4

2 tablespoons safflower oil
3 cloves garlic, minced
1 tablespoon mild honey
2 tablespoons dry white wine
1-2 tablespoons tomato paste, to taste
16 small leeks, white part only, sliced about 1 inch thick
3 sprigs fresh thyme
2 tablespoons lemon juice
Sea salt and freshly ground black pepper

1. Heat oil in a heavy, wide frying pan and add garlic. Sauté about 3 minutes, until golden, and add honey and white wine. Stir together well and add tomato paste. Cook together for a few seconds, and stir in leeks.

2. Cook leeks over medium heat, stirring, about 3 minutes. Add thyme and lemon juice, reduce heat, cover, and cook gently 10 to 15 minutes, stirring from time to time. If pan begins to dry out, add a little wine or water. Add sea salt and freshly ground pepper to taste and remove from heat. Serve warm or at room temperature.

Purée of Sweet Potatoes with Apple

Serves 4

1 pound sweet potatoes
1 pound apples
½ cup plain yogurt
1 tablespoon mild honey
1 tablespoon lime juice
½ teaspoon cinnamon
Ground cloves and freshly grated nutmeg to taste
2 additional apples, cut in rounds and tossed with lemon juice

1. Preheat oven to 425°F. Bake potatoes in their skins 40 to 45 minutes, or until thoroughly soft. At the same time, bake apples on a buttered baking sheet until soft.
2. Remove baked potatoes from their skins and core baked apples. Purée with yogurt, honey, lime juice, cinnamon, cloves, and nutmeg. Adjust seasonings.
3. Toss apple rounds with lemon juice and spoon or pipe on the sweet potato-apple purée. Serve as a side dish.

Onions Cooked in Red Wine
Serves 6 to 8

This is a dish to make on a day you plan to be home all afternoon.

2 tablespoons safflower or vegetable oil
1 tablespoon butter
2 pounds yellow onions, sliced
2 tablespoons mild honey
1½ cups red wine
Sea salt to taste

1. Heat butter and oil over low heat in a heavy-bottomed, wide frying pan and sauté onions 1 hour, covered, stirring occasionally.
2. Uncover, add honey, and increase heat to medium high. Cook 25 minutes, stirring often, until onions are glazed and golden brown.
3. Reduce heat to low again, add wine and cook, stirring fairly often, 2 to 3 hours. The onions will be very soft, almost a purée, reddish brown and sweet. Add sea salt to taste. It takes a long time, but it's worth the effort. Serve as a side dish.

Cooked Cabbage with Apples

Serves 4 to 6

1-2 tablespoons safflower or vegetable oil, as needed
1 onion, sliced
½ medium head red cabbage, shredded
2 cooking apples, peeled and sliced
2 tablespoons raisins
2 tablespoons mild honey
2 tablespoons red wine vinegar
½ teaspoon cinnamon (more to taste)
½ teaspoon allspice
½ teaspoon ground cloves
6 tablespoons plain low-fat yogurt

1. Heat safflower oil in a large, heavy-bottomed frying pan and brown onion.
2. Add red cabbage and apples and sauté about 3 minutes, stirring. Add raisins, honey, vinegar, cinnamon, allspice, and cloves and cook over medium heat, stirring from time to time, about 5 to 10 minutes. Remove from heat, let cool a moment, and stir in yogurt. Or transfer to a serving dish and then stir in yogurt. Serve with bulghur, couscous, or millet.

Baked Acorn Squash
Serves 4 to 6

2-3 small acorn squash
2 tablespoons butter
2 tablespoons mild honey
Ground cinnamon to taste
2 apples, cut in rounds
Safflower oil for the baking dish
½ cup water

1. Preheat oven to 375°F. Cut acorn squash in half lengthwise and remove seeds and stringy pulp.
2. Divide butter and honey evenly among the halves of squash, placing a little pat of butter and a dab of honey in each one. Sprinkle with cinnamon.
3. Place acorn squash in a lightly oiled baking dish and layer rounds of apple across the tops. Add water to the dish, cover with foil or a lid, and bake in preheated oven 1 hour, or until tender.

Fruit Curry

Serves 6 to 8

1 tablespoon butter
1 tablespoon safflower or peanut oil
1 tablespoon curry powder
1 teaspoon freshly grated ginger or ½ teaspoon ground dried
2 bananas, sliced
2 apples, sliced
2 pears, sliced
½ cup chopped, dried figs
½ cup broken, raw cashews
¼ cup Brazil nuts, coarsely chopped
½ cup raisins
½ cup apple juice
2 tablespoons mild honey
½ cup plain yogurt

1. Heat butter and oil together over a medium flame in a wide frying pan or a wok and add curry powder and ginger. Cook about a minute, and add fruit, one kind at a time, tossing gently each time to coat with oil and butter. Add figs, nuts, and raisins. Continue tossing until mixture begins to bubble.
2. Add honey and apple juice, stir together, cover, and reduce heat to low. Simmer 20 to 30 minutes, stirring occasionally to prevent sticking.
3. Remove from heat, transfer to a serving dish, and stir in yogurt. Serve at once over hot, cooked grains.

Baked Beans with Fruit

Serves 6 to 8

1 pound dried white beans or soybeans, washed and picked over
1 quart water
1½ teaspoons sea salt
1½ teaspoons dry mustard
1 onion, chopped
2 apples, sliced
½ cup dried apricots
½ cup mild honey
4 tablespoons molasses

1. Soak beans in water overnight, or for at least several hours. Drain and combine with same quantity of water in a large saucepan. Bring to a boil, add 1 teaspoon sea salt, and cook about 1 to 1½ hours, until tender but not mushy. Drain, reserving 1 cup of liquid.
2. In a small bowl, dissolve mustard in bean liquid and combine with finely chopped onion and salt and pepper to taste. Stir this into beans, along with fresh and dried fruit.
3. Preheat oven to 325°F. Oil a 2 quart casserole or baking dish.
4. Pour bean mixture into prepared casserole. Combine honey and molasses and pour evenly over top.
5. Cover and bake 1 hour, then remove cover and bake another 30 minutes. Serve steaming hot, with Cornbread (page 47).

Pumpkin Stuffed with Millet and Fruit

Serves 8 to 10

This is a delightful substitute for turkey if you are doing a meatless Christmas dinner. It also makes a fine side dish.

2 cups raw millet, cooked
1 cup raisins
Sherry to cover the raisins
1 large pumpkin, about 14 inches in diameter
3 ounces butter, in all
¾ pound apples, peeled and sliced
¾ pound pears, peeled and sliced
¾ cup slivered almonds
½ cup dried apricots, chopped
4 tablespoons mild honey
½-1 teaspoon cinnamon
½ teaspoon nutmeg
½ teaspoon mace
½ teaspoon allspice
½ teaspoon cardamom
½ teaspoon freshly ground black pepper
Sea salt to taste
2 eggs, beaten (optional)
Fresh autumn-colored flowers, for garnish

1. Cook millet, and while doing so soak raisins in sherry to cover. Drain raisins after 30 minutes.
2. Preheat oven to 325°F.
3. Cut out top of pumpkin and remove all seeds and strings. Using a spoon, carefully scrape out a layer of the flesh from the inside of the pumpkin, being careful not to break through the outside. Remove about 1 lb and dice. Steam until tender, about 10 minutes, and set aside.

4. Heat 2 tablespoons of butter in a large, heavy frying pan and sauté apples, pears, almonds, and apricots about 5 minutes. Add 2 tablespoons honey, spices, cooked millet, steamed pumpkin, and sea salt to taste, and cook together another few minutes, stirring. Correct seasonings. Remove from heat. Mix in optional eggs.
5. Melt remaining butter and stir in remaining honey. Add a little cinnamon and brush inside of pumpkin with this. Spoon filling into pumpkin and replace lid. Place on an oiled baking sheet or in a large baking dish and bake 1 hour in preheated oven. Place on a large serving platter, surround with flowers, and serve.

CHAPTER V

DAIRY PRODUCTS AND EGGS

Fines Herbes Butter

4 ounces unsalted butter
1 small clove garlic, minced or puréed (or pressed)
1 teaspoon minced shallot
1 teaspoon minced chives
1 teaspoon thyme
1 tablespoon minced, fresh parsley
1 tablespoon minced, fresh basil or tarragon
Sea salt to taste

1. Chop herbs finely. Let butter come to room temperature and blend in herbs.
2. Transfer to a mold or an attractive butter dish and refrigerate. Soften slightly before serving.

Quiche Aux Fines Herbes

For the crust:
1 cup whole wheat flour
½ teaspoon sea salt
4 ounces unsalted butter
1-3 tablespoons ice cold water
For the quiche:
1 tablespoon safflower oil
1 onion, chopped
½ heaping cup fines herbes (parsley, chives, basil, chervil, tarragon, thyme)
4 eggs, beaten
¾ cup milk
2 tablespoons powdered milk
4 ounces Gruyère cheese, grated
1 ounce Parmesan, grated
Sea salt and freshly ground pepper

1. Make crust. Mix together flour and salt and cut in butter. Add water as needed, gather into a ball, wrap in plastic wrap, and refrigerate 1 to 2 hours or, even better, overnight.

2. Preheat oven to 350°F. Roll out pie crust and line a buttered 10-inch quiche or pie pan. Bake the weighted crust 5 minutes and remove from oven.

3. Heat safflower oil in a frying pan and sauté onion until tender. Remove from heat and stir into beaten eggs, along with herbs. Mix together fresh and powdered milk and stir into egg mixture. Add cheeses and salt and pepper to taste.

4. Pour this mixture into prebaked pie crust and place in preheated oven. Bake 35 to 40 minutes, or until set and beginning to brown on the top. Remove from heat and serve.

Note: This can also be served at room temperature and freezes well.

Illustrated opposite page 112.

Omelette Aux Fines Herbes

1 tablespoon butter
2 eggs
1 teaspoon milk
Sea salt and freshly ground black pepper
1 heaping tablespoon fines herbes (parsley, chives, thyme, basil, or tarragon)
1 sliver garlic, chopped
Additional herbs for garnish (optional)

1. Heat butter in omelette pan, and meanwhile beat eggs together with milk and a little sea salt and freshly ground pepper.
2. When butter stops sizzling, pour in eggs. Keep shaking and tilting the pan with one hand as you gently lift the edges of the omelette with a spatula with the other hand, so that eggs on top can run underneath.
3. As soon as bottom of omelette is set, spread herbs and garlic down the center. Turn omelette and cook another half a minute or so, or until eggs are no longer runny. Turn out onto a plate and serve, garnishing with more herbs if you wish.

Soft-Boiled Eggs with Fines Herbes

1-2 eggs per person

Sea salt and freshly ground black pepper to taste

Chopped, fresh basil and parsley *or* tarragon and parsley
---

1. Bring a pot of water to a boil. Carefully lower eggs into water. Simmer 5 minutes. Remove from pot and run under cold water for about 30 seconds.
2. Clip tops off eggs using a knife or egg cutter. Stand them in egg cups. Lightly salt and pepper if you wish, and sprinkle a teaspoon of herbs over the top of the egg yolk.
3. Serve at once, with toast, and urge eaters to stir the herbs into the yolks.

Herbed Cheese Spread

This should burst forth with the flavors of spring. You can omit some of the herbs if you wish, or substitute others. Use whatever is available.

½ **pound either Ricotta or cream cheese**
4 tablespoons chopped, fresh basil
4 tablespoons chopped, fresh parsley
2 tablespoons chopped, fresh marjoram
1 tablespoon chopped, fresh thyme
3 tablespoons chopped, fresh chives
Juice of ½ lemon
Sea salt and freshly ground black pepper
1 clove garlic, pressed or puréed

1. Using a wooden spoon or mixer, combine all the above ingredients, mixing well. You can also use a food processor for this, but you must be sure to use a plastic blade and not a steel one, or your herbed cheese will become green.
2. Refrigerate until ready to use. Serve as a spread or as a dip. Very nice party fare.

Note: This will keep for two days in the refrigerator.

Brown Rice and Basil Gratin
Serves 6

1 cup raw brown rice, cooked
1 tablespoon butter or safflower oil
½ onion, chopped
1 clove garlic, minced
2 tablespoons pine nuts or sunflower seeds
½ cup basil leaves, chopped
1 cup freshly grated Parmesan or Gruyère cheese
Sea salt and freshly ground black pepper
2 tablespoons whole wheat breadcrumbs

1. Preheat oven to 350°F. Butter a 2 quart baking dish.
2. Heat oil or butter in a frying pan and add onion, garlic, and pine nuts or sunflower seeds. Sauté until onion is tender.
3. Add rice and basil, mix together well, and remove from heat. Add sea salt and freshly ground pepper to taste and stir in cheese.
4. Transfer to baking dish. Top with breadcrumbs and bake 30 minutes.

Note: This can also be used as a stuffing for vegetables. In this case stir in the cheese, then fill the vegetables, sprinkle on the breadcrumbs, and bake as directed above. The dish can also be frozen.

Brown Rice and Basil Eggah

Serves 4 to 6

1 cup raw brown rice, cooked
1 tablespoon butter or safflower oil
½ onion, chopped
1 clove garlic, minced
2 tablespoons pine nuts or sunflower seeds
½ cup basil leaves, chopped
1 cup freshly grated Parmesan or Gruyère cheese
Sea salt and freshly ground black pepper
6 eggs
2 tablespoons butter or safflower oil

1. Follow the directions for Brown Rice and Basil Gratin (see page 111) through to Step 3.
2. Beat eggs in a bowl while you heat butter or oil in a wide frying pan or omelette pan. Stir rice mixture into the eggs.
3. Spread egg and rice mixture over the bottom of the pan. Cook over low heat, shaking the pan gently and lifting occasionally with a spatula so eggs will run underneath, until just about cooked through. This will take about 10 minutes, perhaps a bit longer.
4. Loosen bottom of omelette with a spatula and carefully slide out onto a large plate. Reverse pan over plate and turn omelette back into pan. Cook another 5 minutes or so, until brown on the bottom and cooked through. Remove from heat and serve cut into wedges.

Note: This can also be served cold. It makes good picnic fare.

Opposite: Quiche aux Fines Herbes (page 107).

Baked Ziti with Tomato-Basil Sauce and Cheese

Serves 6 to 8

1 batch Tomato Sauce with Basil (page 144)
Sea salt for pasta water
1 pound Ziti (tubular pasta)
1 tablespoon unsalted butter
1 cup freshly grated Parmesan
1½ cups Ricotta cheese
4 tablespoons breadcrumbs
1 additional tablespoon butter
Sea salt for pasta water

1. Make Tomato Sauce.
2. Preheat oven to 375°F.
3. Bring a large pot of water to a rolling boil, add salt, and cook pasta *al dente* Drain and toss with a tablespoon of butter and half the Parmesan.
4. Oil a 3 quart baking dish or casserole and spread a third of the ziti over the bottom. Top with a third of the Ricotta, a third of the tomato sauce, and a third of the remaining Parmesan. Repeat the layers, ending with the Parmesan. Sprinkle breadcrumbs over the top and dot with remaining butter.
5. Bake 25 to 35 minutes in preheated oven, until bubbling. Remove from heat, let stand 5 minutes, and serve.

Chive Crêpes

Makes about 24 crêpes

These crêpes can also be made with other herbs. Try them with chervil, parsley, dill, or a mixture. They can be filled or served as a side dish.

4 eggs
1 cup milk
1 cup water
½ teaspoon sea salt (more to taste)
1 cup sifted unbleached white flour
1 cup sifted whole wheat pastry flour
4 tablespoons melted butter
6 tablespoons minced chives
Freshly ground black pepper (optional)
Butter for the pan

1. Place eggs, milk, water, and sea salt in blender jar and turn on blender. While blender is running add flours and melted butter. Blend at high speed 1 minute. Transfer to a bowl and refrigerate 2 hours, covered.
2. Stir chives into crêpe batter.
3. Heat a crêpe pan or 6 to 8 inch omelette pan (a cast iron crêpe pan is preferable) over a medium-high flame and brush with butter. Just when butter begins to smoke, lift pan from heat and ladle in about 3 tablespoons crêpe batter. Swirl pan as soon as you pour in batter, to coat evenly (don't be too upset if you don't get this right at first, or if there are holes in the crêpe). Return to heat and cook crêpe about 1 to 1½ minutes. Shake pan to loosen crêpe, or lift gently with a butter knife or spatula. I usually loosen crêpe by sliding a butter knife all the way around the edge, then lift crêpe with my fingers. Don't force crêpe; if it sticks, it isn't ready to turn. It should be golden brown and come away from the pan easily. Turn crêpe and cook about 30 seconds on the other side. Turn out onto a plate.
4. You shouldn't have to butter the crêpe pan between each crêpe after the first one or two. I usually add a little butter after about 5 crêpes, just a small amount, on the end of a brush or a paper towel. Continue to make crêpes until you use up all the batter.
5. If serving crêpes plain, brush with a small amount of herb butter or unsalted plain butter, fold in half with the second side you cooked (the less cooked

side) on the *inside* and the pretty brown side on the outside, and fold in half again, to make a kind of triangle. Place in a buttered baking dish, cover and keep in a warm oven until ready to serve. Or fill with the filling of your choice (ratatouille, creamed spinach, cheese, cheese and egg, leftover vegetables, etc.), roll up, and heat through in a medium oven.

Note: If not using right away, store by stacking between pieces of waxed paper to prevent sticking. Wrap in a plastic bag, or in plastic and foil, and refrigerate or freeze.

Scrambled Eggs with Chives
Serves 4

This is one of the simplest and best ways to enjoy chives. The trick with scrambled eggs is to cook them slowly, over very low heat, so that they become custardy rather than hard. It is easy to produce creamy scrambled eggs without any cream and with very little butter.

1-2 tablespoons butter
8 eggs, beaten
Sea salt and freshly ground black pepper
2-4 tablespoons chopped chives, to taste

1. Melt butter over very low heat in a wide frying pan as you beat eggs about 30 times in a bowl. Add salt, pepper, and chives to the eggs.

2. Add eggs to pan. Stir gently over low heat. Nothing will happen for the first few minutes, then they will begin to stick to the bottom of the pan. Keep stirring eggs up from the bottom of the pan, and continue to cook and stir until eggs reach the desired consistency. Take the pan off the heat from time to time so that eggs do not cook too fast.

3. As soon as you see that the eggs have reached the consistency you want, transfer them to warm plates or a serving dish. They will continue to cook in the pan, so you might remove them from the heat just a second or two before you think they are done. Serve at once.

Mediterranean Sandwich Loaf

Serves 4

- 1 hard-crusted baguette
- ¾ pound tomatoes, seeded and chopped
- 2 hard-boiled eggs, chopped
- ½ cup chopped, fresh parsley
- 2 tablespoons chopped, fresh basil
- 1 teaspoon chopped, fresh thyme
- 1-2 tablespoons chopped, fresh mint, to taste
- 3 shallots, thinly sliced
- 1-2 cloves garlic, to taste, chopped or pressed
- 1 heaping tablespoon capers (more to taste)
- 1 tablespoon wine vinegar
- 2 tablespoons olive oil
- Sea salt and freshly ground black pepper

1. Cut off the ends of the bread and using a long sharp knife, or a spoon, hollow out the loaf, leaving about ½ inch of crust. Save bread that you remove, and pulverize in a food processor or blender.
2. Mix together breadcrumbs with remaining ingredients and season to taste with sea salt and freshly ground pepper. Stuff back into hollowed-out bread. I use the handle of a pestle to stuff it in. There may be some filling remaining, and it makes a delicious addition to a salad, so refrigerate it in a covered bowl.
3. Wrap bread tightly in plastic wrap and foil, and refrigerate at least 8 hours. To serve, slice into 2 inch slices with a serrated knife. This is great summer picnic food.

Illustrated opposite page 16.

Coucou à l'Iranien
Serves 6

A "Coucou" is an Iranian omelette, which is made like a Spanish omelette, flat. It is packed with herbs, and the nuts give it an interesting crunchy texture. I learned it from my French friend Christine, who learned it from her Iranian architect.

2 large bunches parsley, coarsely chopped, or 1 bunch parsley, 1 bunch chervil
1-2 bunches mint, to taste, coarsely chopped
½ teaspoon saffron
12 eggs, beaten
Sea salt and freshly ground black pepper
12 walnuts, shelled and coarsely chopped
12 almonds, coarsely chopped
1 tablespoon olive oil
1 tablespoon vegetable or peanut oil

1. Combine herbs, saffron, eggs, sea salt, pepper, and nuts in a bowl and let sit 30 minutes.
2. Heat olive and vegetable oils together in a wide omelette pan or frying pan and add egg mixture. Cover with a large plate and let cook over low heat 10 minutes, or until almost cooked through.
3. Heat the broiler and finish omelette under the broiler, until it is browned on top and puffed. Can be served hot or at room temperature, cut into wedges. Serve with a green salad.

Provençal Pizza

For the crust:

1 cup whole wheat pastry flour
½ teaspoon sea salt
1 teaspoon baking powder
½ teaspoon baking soda
½ cup water, as needed
2 tablespoons olive oil

For the pizza:

1 tablespoon olive oil
2-3 cloves garlic, minced
2 pounds tomatoes, seeded, chopped
½-1 teaspoon marjoram or oregano
½ teaspoon thyme
¼ cup grated Gruyère cheese
Handful of black nicoise olives
¼ cup sliced mushrooms
2 tablespoons olive oil
Additional herbs of your choice

1. Make crust. Mix together flours, salt, baking powder, and baking soda. Add water and work in with your hands, then add olive oil and work it in. Oil a 10 inch pie pan, quiche pan, or pizza pan with olive oil. Roll out the crust ¼ inch thick and line the pan. Pinch a lip around the edge of the crust. Refrigerate until ready to assemble the pizza.

2. Heat 1 tablespoon olive oil in a heavy-bottomed frying pan or saucepan and sauté garlic 1 minute. Add tomatoes and cook over a medium flame ½ hour. Season to taste with sea salt and freshly ground pepper.

3. Preheat oven to 450°F. Spread tomato sauce over crust, then sprinkle with herbs, grated Gruyère, olives, mushrooms, and additional herbs of your choice. Drizzle olive oil over all.

4. Bake in preheated oven 15 minutes, or until crust is brown and crisp.

Illustrated opposite page 160.

Sorrel Omelette

Makes 1 omelette

1 bunch, or about ¼ pound sorrel
2 tablespoons butter
Sea salt and freshly ground black pepper
2 tablespoons plain yogurt
2 eggs
1 teaspoon milk

1. Wash and stem sorrel. Heat one tablespoon of butter in a frying pan or in your omelette pan and sauté sorrel until it wilts. This should only take a minute or two. The sorrel will lose its bright green color. Add salt and freshly ground pepper to taste, remove from heat, and stir in yogurt.
2. Heat remaining butter in omelette pan and meanwhile beat eggs together with milk and a little salt and freshly ground pepper.
3. When butter stops sizzling pour in eggs. Keep shaking and tilting pan with one hand as you gently lift the edges of the omelette with a spatula with the other hand, so that eggs on top can run underneath.
4. As soon as bottom of omelette is solid, spread sorrel down the middle. Turn omelette and cook for another half a minute or so, or until eggs are no longer runny; turn out onto a plate and serve.

Spinach Gnocchi with Sage Butter

Serves 6

1½ pounds fresh spinach or 2 10-ounce packages frozen
2 tablespoons butter
8 ounces Ricotta cheese
Sea salt and freshly ground black pepper
Pinch of nutmeg
2 eggs, beaten
3 tablespoons unbleached flour
½ cup freshly grated Parmesan
1-2 additional tablespoons unbleached white flour
4½ quarts water
4 tablespoons unsalted butter
10 leaves fresh sage, sliced

1. If you use fresh spinach, wash and stem, blanch and squeeze out excess water. Chop fine. Allow frozen spinach to thaw and squeeze out excess water. Chop fine.

2. Heat first 2 tablespoons butter in a saucepan over very low heat and add spinach, Ricotta, sea salt, and pepper to taste, and a little nutmeg. Using a wooden spoon, stir and mix together well, and cook 5 minutes. Remove from heat and stir in beaten eggs, 3 tablespoons flour, and 5 tablespoons of the Parmesan. Refrigerate at least 2 hours, or until stiff enough to handle.

3. Place additional flour on a plate. Take up the spinach-Ricotta mixture by heaped teaspoons (you can make them larger than this if you like) and roll them in flour, forming little balls coated with flour.

4. Bring water to a boil in a large pot. Add a heaping tablespoon salt, then drop in gnocchi one by one. When they float to the surface wait 3 to 4 minutes, then remove with a slotted spoon and set aside.

5. Melt remaining 4 tablespoons butter in a wide frying pan and add sage. Sauté about 2 minutes, then add gnocchi. Heat through, tossing gently with a wooden spoon to coat thoroughly with butter, and transfer to a warm serving dish. Sprinkle with remaining Parmesan and serve.

Cheese, Bread, and Tomato Casserole

Serves 6 to 8

4-6 slices whole wheat bread
8 ounces Cheddar cheese, grated
3 ripe tomatoes, sliced
4 eggs
2 cups milk
2 tablespoons dry white wine
½ teaspoon thyme, dried or fresh
½ teaspoon dry mustard
Lots of freshly ground black pepper
Sea salt to taste

1. Preheat oven to 350°F. Butter a 2 quart baking dish or soufflé dish.
2. Layer bread, cheese, and tomatoes in that order, two layers of each in prepared baking dish.
3. Beat together eggs, milk, wine, thyme, mustard, pepper, and salt. Pour over cheese, bread, and tomatoes.
4. Bake 35 to 45 minutes, or until puffed and browned.

Sweet Potato Soufflé

The honey here accentuates the marvelous natural sweetness of the potatoes.

2 pounds sweet potatoes or yams
½ pound cooking apples
2 tablespoons melted butter
2 tablespoons mild honey
Juice of 1 large lime
½ cup plain yogurt
4 eggs, separated
Pinch of sea salt

1. Preheat oven to 425°F. Brush sweet potatoes with oil, pierce them, and bake 40 minutes, or until thoroughly soft. Halfway through baking add apples and bake until soft. Remove from oven and when cool enough to handle, peel sweet potatoes and peel and core apples. Turn oven down to 375°F.
2. Butter a 2 quart soufflé dish.
3. Purée potatoes and apples through the fine blade of a food mill. Mix in butter, lime juice, honey, and yogurt (this can also be done in a food processor). Beat egg yolks and stir in.
4. Beat egg whites until they begin to foam and add sea salt. Continue to beat until they form stiff peaks. Stir one-quarter of beaten egg whites into sweet potato purée, and gently fold in rest. Carefully spoon mixture into prepared soufflé dish.
5. Bake 30 minutes in preheated oven. It should be beginning to brown on top. Serve at once.

CHAPTER VI

SALADS

Beet Salad

Serves 4

1 pound raw beets
2 tablespoons chopped, fresh parsley or dill
1 cup plain yogurt
1 clove garlic, puréed or put through a press
1 teaspoon crushed caraway seeds
Sea salt and freshly ground black pepper

1. Steam beets until tender, 15 to 30 minutes, depending on size of beets. Drain, run under cold water, and remove skin. Slice thinly, and toss with parsley or dill.
2. Mix together yogurt, garlic, caraway seeds, sea salt, and freshly ground pepper. Toss with beets and serve, or chill and serve.

Tomato and Mozzarella Salad with Pesto

Serves 4 to 6

½ recipe Pesto (page 78)
4 additional tablespoons olive oil
4-6 firm, ripe, medium-sized tomatoes
4 ounces Mozzarella cheese
Freshly ground black pepper
Fresh basil leaves for garnish
Watercress or lettuce leaves for lining plates

1. Make pesto and set aside (freeze half if you make a whole batch).
2. Stir additional olive oil into pesto you are using.
3. Slice tomatoes in thin lengthwise slices, from stem end down to within about ¼ inch of bottom.
4. Slice Mozzarella very thin, and insert between tomato slices. Grind some pepper over the top.
5. Line individual salad plates with lettuce leaves or watercress. Place tomatoes on top and drizzle on pesto. Serve.

Illustrated opposite page 128.

Caraway Coleslaw

Serves 6 to 8

½ medium head green cabbage, finely shredded
2 apples, grated
2 stalks celery, thinly sliced
½ medium onion, grated
1 teaspoon crushed caraway seeds
1 carrot, grated (optional)
¼ cup cider vinegar
½ cup mild honey
1½ cups plain yogurt
¼ cup lemon juice
Freshly ground black pepper

1. Prepare vegetables and apples and toss together in a bowl, along with crushed caraway seeds.
2. Heat honey and cider vinegar together in a small saucepan, just until honey dissolves into vinegar. Add lemon juice. Remove from heat and stir in yogurt. Mix well.
3. Toss dressing with cabbage mixture. Add freshly ground pepper to taste, cover, and refrigerate overnight.

Middle Eastern Beet Salad

Serves 6

2 pounds uncooked beets, trimmed
Juice of 1 lemon
½ teaspoon cumin
½ teaspoon paprika
¼ teaspoon cinnamon
1 tablespoon orange flower water
2 tablespoons olive oil
2 tablespoons chopped, fresh parsley
Sea salt to taste
Leaf or romaine lettuce

1. Wash beets and place on a plate in a steamer. Steam until tender, about 20 to 30 minutes. Set aside liquid that accumulates on the plate and refresh beets under cold water. Peel and slice.
2. Toss beets with lemon juice, cumin, paprika, cinnamon, orange flower water, olive oil, half the parsley, and sea salt to taste. Add liquid from plate and toss again. Taste and adjust seasonings. Cover and chill.
3. Line a bowl or platter with lettuce leaves, arrange beets on top of these, sprinkle with parsley, and serve.

Lebanese Eggplant Salad
Serves 4 to 6

1 pound eggplant
Olive oil
3 tablespoons tahini
Juice of 1 lemon
1-2 cloves garlic, minced or pressed
Cayenne to taste (1-2 pinches)
Sea salt to taste
Fresh, chopped parsley for garnish
1 red or green pepper, sliced in wide strips

1. Preheat oven to 450°F. Cut eggplant in half lengthwise and score with a sharp knife down the middle, to the skin but not through it. Oil a baking sheet with olive oil and place eggplant on it, cut side down. Bake in the hot oven 15 to 20 minutes, or until thoroughly soft and the skin is shrivelled. Remove from oven and allow to cool.
2. Scoop the eggplant out from skin and mash in a mortar and pestle, or in a food processor. Blend in tahini, lemon juice, garlic, cayenne, and sea salt. Place in an attractive bowl and sprinkle with parsley. Chill.
3. Serve, using strips of green or red peppers as scoopers.

Pilaki (Turkish Cooked Vegetable Salad)

Serves 4

2 tablespoons safflower oil
2 medium onions, sliced
2 cloves garlic, minced or pressed
2 medium tomatoes, sliced
4 medium green peppers, sliced
1/2 teaspoon cumin seeds
1/8 teaspoon cayenne (can use less)
3/4 cup water
Sea salt to taste
Juice of 1/2-1 lemon, to taste

1. Heat oil in a wide frying pan and add onions and garlic. Sauté a few minutes, until onions begin to soften. Add tomatoes, green peppers, and cumin seeds. Sauté about 5 minutes.
2. Stir in water, reduce heat, add cayenne, and simmer until vegetables are soft and water evaporated, about 15 minutes. Stir from time to time.
3. Add salt to taste and chill. Just before serving, stir in lemon juice.

Opposite: Tomato and Mozzarella Salad with Pesto (page 124).

Salade Mesclun
(Mixed Greens Salad)

Serves 4 to 6

½ pound mixed tender bitter greens, such as lamb's lettuce, chicory, dandelion greens, nasturtium, oak leaf lettuce, watercress
1 ounce chervil, stems included
2 tablespoons good quality wine vinegar
Sea salt and freshly ground black pepper
1 small clove garlic (optional)
½ teaspoon Dijon mustard (optional)
6 tablespoons olive oil *or* 4 tablespoons safflower oil and 2 tablespoons walnut oil

1. Wash all the greens well and dry. Toss greens and chervil together.
2. Combine vinegar, sea salt and pepper, the optional garlic and mustard, and the oil or oils. Mix together well and toss with salad. Serve at once.

Salade Verte Aux Champignons

Serves 4 to 6

1 head Boston lettuce
A large handful of watercress
¼ pound mushrooms, cleaned and sliced
1 tablespoon snipped chervil
2 tablespoons wine vinegar
½ teaspoon Dijon mustard
Sea salt and freshly ground black pepper
2 tablespoons safflower oil
4 tablespoons olive oil

1. Wash lettuce and watercress well and dry. Toss together with mushrooms and chervil.
2. Combine vinegar, mustard, sea salt, and pepper. Whisk in oils and mix well. Toss with salad just before serving.

Cacik

Serves 3 to 4

1 cup plain low-fat yogurt
1 tablespoon chopped chives
Pinch of sea salt
Juice of ½ lemon
1 clove garlic, puréed (optional)
1 medium cucumber, sliced thin and diced
4 radishes, thinly sliced
2 sprigs mint, for garnish

1. Combine yogurt, chives, salt, lemon juice, and optional garlic and beat together. Stir in cucumber and radishes and stir together. Chill several

hours. Garnish with mint leaves.
2. Serve as a salad or side dish, or as a garnish for a soup.

Carottes Rapées (Grated Carrot Salad)

Serves 4 to 6

This is a very simple French salad, and one of my favorites.

2 pounds carrots
2 tablespoons chopped chives
1-2 tablespoons chopped fresh parsley
Juice of ½ lemon
1 tablespoon wine vinegar
1 small clove garlic, minced
1 teaspoon Dijon mustard
Sea salt and freshly ground black pepper
8 tablespoons olive oil, or a mixture of olive oil and safflower oil

1. Grate carrots fine, either with a hand grater or a food processor. Toss them with chives and parsley.
2. Combine lemon juice, vinegar, garlic, Dijon mustard, salt, and pepper and mix together well. Whisk in oil or oils and toss with carrots. Serve at once or chill and serve, tossing once more just before serving.

Melon, Cucumber, and Tomato Salad

Serves 6

This may seem strange at first glance, but it works quite well.

For the salad:
1 large cucumber, peeled and diced
1 pound ripe tomatoes
1 honeydew melon
1 tablespoon chopped, fresh parsley
1 tablespoon chopped, fresh mint
1½ tablespoons chopped chives
For the dressing:
3 tablespoons wine vinegar
½-1 teaspoon mild honey
Sea salt and freshly ground black pepper
6 tablespoons safflower or vegetable oil
Fresh watercress for garnish

1. Salt cucumber pieces and let sit 1 hour.
2. Peel and seed tomatoes and cut into wedges, and peel melon and cut into 1 inch dice, or make into balls.
3. Rinse cucumber thoroughly and toss together with melon and tomatoes.
4. Mix together vinegar, honey, sea salt, and freshly ground pepper. Whisk in oil and toss with salad mixture. Place in a glass salad bowl and chill 1 to 2 hours.
5. Just before serving toss with herbs. Garnish with watercress and serve.

Lentil Salad

Serves 6

1 tablespoon safflower or vegetable oil
1 onion, chopped
2 cloves garlic, minced or pressed
1 pound lentils, washed
Water to cover lentils by 2 inches
1 bay leaf
3 tablespoons wine vinegar
1 additional clove garlic, puréed
½ teaspoon Dijon mustard
1 teaspoon ground cumin
Sea salt and freshly ground black pepper
½ cup olive oil
Cooking liquid from the lentils
1 red onion, minced
½ bunch chopped, fresh parsley
Leaf lettuce and tomatoes for garnish

1. Heat safflower or vegetable oil in a heavy-bottomed saucepan and sauté onion and 1 clove garlic until onion is tender. Add lentils, water, the remaining clove of garlic, and the bay leaf. Bring to a boil, reduce heat, cover, and cook until lentils are tender, about 45 minutes. Remove the bay leaf. Remove from heat and drain, retaining liquid.

2. Mix together vinegar, additional garlic, mustard, cumin, salt, and freshly ground pepper. Whisk in olive oil. Add cooking liquid from lentils to taste.

3. Toss dressing with lentils and stir in red onion and parsley. Cover and chill. Serve over a bed of lettuce leaves, with sliced tomatoes for garnish.

Middle Eastern Salad

Serves 4 to 6

½ medium cucumber, cubed
4 spring onions, thinly sliced
4 tomatoes, chopped
1 green or red pepper, diced
1 bunch watercress, chopped
2 tablespoons chopped, fresh dill

For the dressing:

3 tablespoons lemon juice
1 clove garlic, minced or pressed
2 tablespoons yogurt
Sea salt and freshly ground black pepper
¼ cup olive oil

1. Toss together all the ingredients for the salad.
2. Mix together lemon juice, garlic, yogurt, sea salt, and pepper and whisk in olive oil.
3. Toss salad with dressing and serve. You may chill this for an hour or so, but no longer.

Fresh Dilled Cucumbers

Serves 6 to 8

2 long or 3 shorter cucumbers, peeled and cut into spears
2 red onions, sliced thin
3 cloves garlic, sliced
3 cups water
1 cup cider or white wine vinegar
4 heaping tablespoons chopped, fresh dill
½ cup safflower or olive oil
Sea salt and freshly ground black pepper

1. Prepare vegetables and set aside.
2. Combine remaining ingredients, stir together well, and toss with cucumbers, onions, and garlic in a large bowl. Cover and refrigerate overnight. Add more sea salt, pepper, and vinegar if you wish.

Note: This keeps several days in the refrigerator.

Romaine and Mushroom Salad with Fennel

Serves 4 to 6

1 head romaine lettuce
1 thick-skinned lemon
1 teaspoon crushed fennel seeds
¼ pound mushrooms, sliced
2 tablespoons chopped, fresh fennel
Radishes for garnish
For the dressing:
Juice of ½ lemon
1-2 tablespoons tarragon vinegar
¼ teaspoon dry mustard
Sea salt and freshly ground black pepper
½ teaspoon honey
3 tablespoons safflower oil
3 tablespoons cream or buttermilk

1. Separate lettuce leaves, wash, and slice crosswise.
2. Using a lemon peeler or sharp knife, pare rind from half the lemon and trim away any white part. Slice into very fine shreds, blanch, and drain.
3. Cut away white pith from lemon by working a serrated knife around in a spiral with a sawing motion, the blade angled in slightly. Now cut away thin slices of lemon from in between membranes. Toss these with romaine, fennel seeds, mushrooms, and chopped fennel.
4. Combine lemon juice, vinegar, mustard, salt, pepper, and honey. Whisk in oil, then cream or buttermilk. Adjust seasonings, toss with salad, and serve, garnishing with radishes.

Mushroom and Fennel Salad with Lime Vinaigrette

Serves 4 to 6

¾ pound mushrooms
2 tablespoons minced spring onions
1 avocado, diced
3 tablespoons chopped fennel
Boston or leaf lettuce
Radishes for garnish

For the dressing:

4 tablespoons fresh lime juice
1 small clove garlic, pressed or puréed
Sea salt and freshly ground black pepper
8 tablespoons olive or vegetable oil, or a combination

1. Trim stems of mushrooms and wipe with a damp towel. If they are very sandy rinse quickly under cold water and wipe dry with a towel. Slice very thin.
2. Toss together mushrooms, minced spring onion, fennel, and avocado.
3. Mix together lime juice, garlic, sea salt, and pepper and whisk in oil or oils. Toss with mushrooms.
4. Line a salad bowl or platter with lettuce leaves and fill with mushrooms. Garnish with radishes and serve.

Tossed Salad with Marjoram
Serves 6

1 head Boston lettuce, or a mixture of different young lettuces
½ small cucumber, peeled if waxed and thinly sliced
6 large radishes, sliced
5 mushrooms, cleaned and sliced
½ sweet red pepper, sliced thin
2 tablespoons chopped, fresh marjoram
4 spring onions, thinly sliced
For the dressing:
Juice of ½ lemon
2 tablespoons wine or cider vinegar
1 small clove garlic, puréed
½-1 teaspoon Dijon mustard
Sea salt and freshly ground black pepper
¼ teaspoon dried tarragon
⅓ cup safflower or vegetable oil
⅓ cup olive oil

1. Wash lettuce and pat dry. Toss with remaining salad ingredients.
2. Mix together lemon juice, vinegar, garlic, mustard, sea salt, pepper, and tarragon. Whisk in the two oils and combine well.
3. Toss dressing with salad just before serving.

Zucchini with Yogurt and Mint

Serves 4

1 pound zucchini
1½ cups plain yogurt
2-3 tablespoons chopped mint
Sea salt to taste

1. Cut zucchini into spears and steam 5 to 10 minutes, to taste. Refresh under cold water and pat dry.
2. Toss steamed zucchini with yogurt and mint. Add sea salt to taste. Refrigerate until ready to serve.

Cucumber Salad with Feta Cheese Dressing

Serves 4

Juice of 1 lemon
1 small clove garlic, minced or pressed
½ teaspoon crushed dried oregano
4 tablespoons olive oil
Freshly ground black pepper
4 ounces Feta cheese, crumbled
1 long cucumber, thinly sliced
1 mild red onion, thinly sliced
Leaf lettuce
A handful of black Greek olives

1. Mix together lemon juice, garlic, and oregano. Whisk in olive oil and add freshly ground pepper to taste. Crumble in Feta.
2. Toss dressing with cucumbers and onions. Line a platter with lettuce leaves and top with salad. Garnish with olives and serve, or chill and serve.

Moroccan Carrot Salad
Serves 4

1 pound carrots, peeled and sliced
1 cup water
Sea salt to taste
4 cloves garlic, crushed
½ bunch fresh parsley, finely chopped
1 teaspoon cumin
¼-½ teaspoon chopped, hot chili pepper
3 tablespoons vegetable oil
3 tablespoons lemon juice

1. Steam carrots above water 10 minutes. Refresh under cold water and retain steaming liquid.
2. Pound salt, garlic, parsley, cumin, and hot chili pepper together in a mortar until you obtain a thick paste.
3. Heat vegetable oil in a frying pan and add paste. Sauté about 3 minutes and stir in ¼ to ½ cup of the cooking water from carrots. Bring mixture to a boil, stirring, then pour into a bowl. Add carrots and toss with lemon juice. Adjust seasonings, refrigerate several hours, and serve.

Spinach and Bulghur Salad with Poppy Seed Dressing

Serves 6

1½ cups bulghur
3 cups boiling water
½ pound spinach, washed and chopped
4 ounces tofu, crumbled
2 tablespoons sesame seeds
1 tablespoon chopped, fresh mint
1 recipe Poppy Seed Dressing (page 152)

1. Place bulghur in a bowl and pour on boiling water. Let sit 30 minutes, or until water is absorbed and bulghur is soft. Meanwhile make Poppy Seed Dressing. If bulghur on top is not absorbing enough water, toss from time to time. Drain off excess water when bulghur is tender and squeeze dry in a towel.

2. Toss bulghur with remaining ingredients, including Poppy Seed Dressing, and chill until ready to serve.

Red Cabbage and Apple Salad with Poppy Seed Dressing

Serves 4 to 6

1 recipe Poppy Seed Dressing (page 152)
1 pound red cabbage, shredded
1 apple, grated
2 tablespoons minced chives
Leaf lettuce for the bowl or platter

1. Make salad dressing.
2. Toss together cabbage, apple, and chives. Toss with dressing.
3. Line a salad bowl or platter with lettuce leaves and fill with salad. Serve, or chill and serve.

Shredded Carrot Salad with Poppy Seed Dressing

Serves 4 to 6

1 recipe Poppy Seed Dressing (page 152)
1 pound carrots, scrubbed and grated
Leaf lettuce for the bowl
3 tablespoons sunflower seeds

1. Make Poppy Seed Dressing and toss with grated carrots.
2. Line a bowl or platter with lettuce leaves and top with carrots. Sprinkle on sunflower seeds and serve, or chill and serve.

CHAPTER VII

SAUCES, DRESSINGS, AND CONDIMENTS

Herb Vinegars

Any number of vinegars can be infused with fresh herbs to give you a variety of salad dressings and sauces. I most often use tarragon and mint for my flavored vinegars, but basil is also good, and fresh coriander and dill make interesting vinegars as well.

1-3 sprigs tarragon, mint, or basil
---
1 quart wine or cider vinegar
---

1. Combine herbs and vinegar in a jar and seal well. Allow to macerate for 2 weeks before using.
2. You can also fill a jar with loosely packed leaves of the herbs, cover with vinegar, macerate for 2 weeks, and strain.

Tomato Sauce with Basil

Makes 5 cups

3 pounds fresh or canned tomatoes*
1 tablespoon olive oil or butter
1 small onion, minced
3 cloves garlic, minced or put through a press
1 tablespoon tomato paste (optional)
2 tablespoons fresh chopped basil
Sea salt and freshly ground black pepper to taste
Pinch of cinnamon (optional)

1. Seed and chop tomatoes.
2. Heat olive oil or butter in a heavy-bottomed wide frying pan or a saucepan and add onion and 2 cloves of the garlic. Sauté a few minutes, or until onion is tender.
3. Add tomatoes, remaining garlic, and tomato paste and bring to a simmer. Turn up heat and cook quickly for 20 minutes, stirring from time to time.
4. Add salt and freshly ground pepper to taste, and the basil. Cook another 5 minutes and taste. If you want a sweeter sauce, add a pinch of cinnamon. Correct salt, pepper, and garlic and remove from heat.
5. Use in pasta dishes or with grains.

*Use fresh tomatoes only if you can find very ripe local tomatoes. Otherwise, canned will yield a much better sauce.

Note: This sauce can be frozen and keeps several days in the refrigerator.

Coriander-Cumin Tomato Sauce

1 large bunch fresh coriander, about 1 ounce
6 heaping tablespoons parsley
1 seeded green chili
2 spring onions or shallots, trimmed
1 large clove garlic
3 tablespoons olive oil
1½ teaspoons ground cumin
1 pound tomatoes, peeled, chopped
1 tablespoon tomato paste
Sea salt to taste

1. Using a blender or food processor with the steel blade, blend together coriander, parsley, chili, spring onions or shallots, garlic, and two tablespoons of olive oil. Set aside.
2. Heat oil in a heavy frying pan and add cumin. Turn heat high, cook a few seconds, and add chopped tomatoes. Cook for 1 to 2 minutes over high heat, stirring or shaking the pan. Stir in tomato paste, cook about half a minute more, and remove from heat. Allow to cool and stir into coriander mixture. Add salt to taste.
3. Cover and refrigerate before serving. Use as a dip or as a hot sauce, or as a dressing with avocados.

Note: This can be frozen and will keep for a few days in the refrigerator.

Coriander Sauce

4-6 pitted prunes
½ cup cooking liquid from the prunes (see Step 1)
4 tablespoons lime juice
¾ cup fresh coriander leaves
½ cup chopped, fresh parsley
¼ cup chopped, fresh basil*
2 cloves garlic, peeled
½ teaspoon chopped, fresh ginger
¼-½ teaspoon sea salt
¼ teaspoon freshly ground black pepper
4 tablespoons sunflower seeds
4 tablespoons walnut or safflower oil

1. Cover prunes with water and bring to a simmer. Simmer ½ hour, or until thoroughly soft. Drain and retain ½ cup of liquid for sauce.
2. Combine all ingredients except oil and cooking liquid from prunes in a blender or food processor fitted with the steel blade and blend together until you have a paste. Without stopping the blender or food processor, blend in oil and liquid. Adjust seasonings. Use as a dip, as a topping for tofu or grains, or as a sauce for vegetables.

*Can use all coriander.

Note: This will last for about 3 days in the refrigerator.

Very Quick, Very Fresh Tomato Sauce

Makes 2 cups

Use only the ripest tomatoes for this sauce. It is a nice accompaniment for eggs or pasta. Also good with vegetables like zucchini, green beans, or eggplant.

1 tablespoon butter or olive oil
1 shallot, minced
1 clove garlic, minced
1 pound tomatoes, peeled and chopped
2 teaspoons chopped fresh marjoram
Sea salt and freshly ground black pepper

Heat butter or oil in a heavy-bottomed frying pan and sauté shallot and garlic gently for 2 minutes, or until shallot is soft. Add tomatoes, turn heat to moderately high, and cook 10 to 15 minutes. Add marjoram and sea salt and freshly ground pepper to taste, remove from heat, and serve.

Note: This can be frozen but in that case cook 30 minutes.

Tomato-Mint Sauce

½ pound ripe tomatoes
1 small clove garlic
2-3 tablespoons fresh mint
4 tablespoons red wine vinegar
4 tablespoons olive or safflower oil
Sea salt and freshly ground black pepper

Blend together tomatoes, garlic, mint, and vinegar in a blender, or mash together in a mortar and pestle until smooth. Drizzle in oil and add sea salt and freshly ground pepper to taste. Chill several hours. This is a tasty salad dressing and can also serve as a sauce for vegetables or as a dip.

Tofu Tomato Sauce

Makes about 1½ quarts

1 tablespoon olive or safflower oil

1 onion, minced

3 cloves garlic, minced or pressed

½ pound tofu

1 tablespoon tamari soy sauce

3 pounds tomatoes, seeded and puréed, or the equivalent canned

3 tablespoons tomato paste

1 teaspoon dried oregano

Pinch of thyme

½ teaspoon mild honey

Sea salt and freshly ground black pepper

Pinch of cinnamon

1. Heat oil in a large, heavy-bottomed frying pan or saucepan and sauté onion with 1 clove of the garlic until onion is tender.
2. Add tofu and more oil if necessary, tamari, and cook, mashing tofu with the back of your spoon, until tofu begins to stick to pan, about 5 to 10 minutes. Add tomatoes and remaining ingredients and bring to a simmer. Cook, covered, 30 minutes. Adjust seasonings.
3. Remove from heat and serve with pasta, grains, or vegetables.

Note: This will keep a few days in the refrigerator but will not freeze.

Tomato-Sage Sauce
Serves 6 to 8

2 tablespoons olive oil
1 onion, chopped
2 small carrots, minced
2-4 cloves garlic, chopped or pressed
4 pounds ripe tomatoes, chopped or the equivalent canned
60 fresh sage leaves (about ½ bunch), tied in a tight bundle
1 teaspoon mild honey
Sea salt and freshly ground black pepper

1. Heat olive oil in a heavy-bottomed saucepan or casserole and add onion, carrots, and half the garlic. Sauté about 5 minutes over medium-low heat. Add tomatoes, remaining garlic, sage leaves, and honey and bring to a simmer. Simmer uncovered 30 minutes. Remove the bundle of sage leaves and add salt and freshly ground pepper to taste.
2. Purée tomato sauce roughly in a food processor or blender or through the wide blade of a food mill. Return to heat 10 minutes. Good with pasta.

Tofu Remoulade Sauce

This makes a spectacular low-fat dressing for vegetable salads. It will keep for up to a week in the refrigerator.

½ pound tofu
½ cup plain yogurt or buttermilk
Juice of 1 lemon
1 small clove garlic
½ teaspoon dry mustard
1 teaspoon tamari soy sauce or miso
Yolks of 2 hardboiled eggs
1 teaspoon chopped tarragon
1 teaspoon chopped chives
1 teaspoon (or more, to taste) capers

Blend all the ingredients except tarragon, chives, and capers together in a blender or food processor until smooth. Stir in herbs and capers. Chill in a covered container.

Blender "Bearnaise"

It is the vinegar reduction which allows me to call this sauce a bearnaise, for it has none of the butter and eggs of a traditional one. It is tart and savory, and goes well with vegetables and grains.

4 tablespoons tarragon vinegar
6 tablespoons minced shallot or spring onion bottoms
3 tablespoons minced carrot
3 tablespoons minced celery
1 large ripe tomato, peeled, seeded, and chopped
2 tablespoons chopped parsley
½ cup vegetable stock
1 tablespoon olive oil
1 teaspoon chopped, fresh tarragon
Sea salt and freshly ground black pepper

1. Combine vinegar, shallot, carrot, and celery in a small, heavy-bottomed saucepan and place over moderate heat. Simmer mixture until almost all of the vinegar has evaporated. There should only be enough left so that vegetables aren't completely dry.

2. Add chopped tomato and continue to cook, stirring occasionally, for about 15 minutes, or until the mixture is almost dry again. About 5 minutes before the end of this cooking, stir in parsley.

3. Remove from heat and transfer to a blender. Blend, along with vegetable stock, until smooth. While blender is running, drizzle in olive oil.

4. Transfer puréed sauce back to saucepan and season to taste with sea salt and freshly ground pepper and tarragon. Heat through gently and serve. This can also be served cold.

Note: This sauce freezes well and will keep for a few days in the refrigerator.

Low-Fat Russian Dressing

This has the same sweet tomatoey taste of a Russian dressing, but it is made with tofu and yogurt instead of mayonnaise, so it has none of the fat. Nor does it have the vast amount of sugar present in ketchup. It makes a fine salad dressing or dip for vegetables.

½ pound tofu
½ cup plain low-fat yogurt
Juice of 1 lemon
½ teaspoon dry mustard
1-2 teaspoons soy sauce, to taste
1 large, ripe tomato, peeled
2 teaspoons mild honey
2 teaspoons cider vinegar
⅛ teaspoon ground cloves
Pinch of cayenne
2 teaspoons tomato paste

Blend all the ingredients together in a blender or food processor until smooth. Refrigerate in a covered container for up to 1 week.

Poppy Seed Dressing

2 tablespoons lemon juice
2 tablespoons vinegar
2 tablespoons plus 1 teaspoon mild honey
2 tablespoons poppy seeds
Pinch of sea salt
Freshly ground black pepper
2 tablespoons safflower oil
⅔ cup plain low-fat yogurt

1. Stir together lemon juice, vinegar, honey, poppy seeds, sea salt, and pepper. Make sure honey is dissolved, and stir in safflower oil and yogurt.

Refrigerate until ready to use.

Note: This will keep for a week in the refrigerator. Use with Spinach and Bulghar Salad (page 141), Red Cabbage and Apple Salad (page 142), and Shredded Carrot Salad (page 142).

Oriental Salad Dressing

2 tablespoons sesame tahini
1 tablespoon mild honey
4 tablespoons vinegar
½ teaspoon grated fresh ginger
1 tablespoon tamari soy sauce
2 tablespoons sesame oil
4 tablespoons water or vegetable stock
3 tablespoons safflower oil
Freshly ground black pepper to taste

Blend all the ingredients together in a blender, or stir together with a fork or whisk until smooth. This is great with vegetable salads and noodle salads and will last a week in the refrigerator.

Homemade Tomato Ketchup

Makes about 1½ quarts

4 quarts ripe, fleshy tomatoes
1 onion, minced
½ medium sweet red pepper, minced
2 cloves garlic, minced or pressed
1 cup cider vinegar
2 teaspoons mustard seeds
2 teaspoons whole allspice
1 stick cinnamon, broken up
1 teaspoon whole black peppercorns
1 bay leaf
½ teaspoon whole cloves
½ teaspoon ground coriander
⅛ teaspoon dried, red pepper flakes
½ cup mild honey

1. Quarter tomatoes and cook over high heat in a large saucepan 30 minutes, stirring occasionally. Measure out a little over 2 quarts of the pulp into a large stainless steel or enameled pot. Add onion, sweet red pepper, garlic, and vinegar and bring to a boil.
2. Tie mustard seeds, allspice, cinnamon, peppercorns, bay leaf, cloves, coriander, and pepper flakes together in a doubled cheesecloth. Add to tomatoes along with honey. Simmer uncovered 1 hour over medium heat, stirring often. Remove cheesecloth bag and squeeze out all the moisture.
3. Purée tomato mixture in a blender, then press through a sieve or put through the fine blade of a food mill. Return to pot and simmer over low heat until mixture is thick enough to mound up slightly on a spoon. It will thicken further upon cooling.
4. Ladle into clean, sterilized jars, leaving ½ inch headspace. Wipe rims and cover with canning jar lids.
5. Put jars on a rack in a kettle half full of boiling water. Add more boiling water to cover the lids by 2 inches. Bring to a hard boil, cover pot, and boil 20 minutes.

6. Remove from boiling water and allow to cool. Let mellow in jars 2 to 4 weeks, and once opened, keep refrigerated. Store unopened jars in a cool, dry place.

Tahini-Tamari Sauce

6 tablespoons tahini
2 tablespoons tamari soy sauce
2 tablespoons warm water
½ teaspoon ground ginger, or 1 teaspoon grated fresh
2 teaspoons mild honey

Combine all the ingredients in a bowl and stir together well. Refrigerate. Use this as a spread for bread or tofu or as a dip for raw vegetables.

Coarse-Ground Mustard with Red Wine and Garlic

It is amazingly easy to make your own mustard, and once you begin you will see how many variations you can come up with. I often make mustards as Christmas gifts. They are always appreciated.

4 heaping tablespoons mustard seeds
2 tablespoons red wine
1/3 cup red wine vinegar
1/4 cup water
1/4 teaspoon ground allspice
1/2-1 teaspoon mild honey, to taste
1/4 teaspoon freshly ground pepper
1/2-1 teaspoon minced garlic, to taste
1 small bay leaf, finely crumbled or ground

1. Combine mustard seeds, red wine, and vinegar in a dish and let stand 3 hours or more.
2. Put mixture into a blender jar or food processor and add remaining ingredients. Purée to a coarse texture.
3. Scrape into the top of a double boiler and stir over simmering water 5 to 10 minutes, or until mixture has thickened somewhat. Scrape into a jar, cool, and refrigerate.

Note: This will keep indefinitely in the refrigerator.

Tarragon Mustard

4 heaping tablespoons mustard seeds
2 tablespoons dry white wine or vermouth
⅓ cup white wine vinegar
2 teaspoons dried tarragon
⅓ cup water
⅛ teaspoon freshly ground pepper
⅛ teaspoon ground allspice
2 teaspoons mild honey

1. Combine mustard seeds, white wine or vermouth, vinegar, and 1 teaspoon of tarragon in a bowl and let stand at least 3 hours.
2. Pour mixture into a blender jar or food processor (a blender does a more thorough job, but you will have to start and stop it to stir the mixture) and add remaining ingredients except additional teaspoon of tarragon. Purée as finely as you can.
3. Scrape mixture into the top part of a double boiler and stir over simmering water about 10 minutes. A layer will stick to the bottom of the pan, but don't worry; it won't burn as long as you are using a double boiler. Cool, add remaining tarragon, and scrape into a jar. Refrigerate.

Note: This will keep indefinitely in the refrigerator.

Orange Peach Dressing

This goes nicely with fruit salads.

3 dried apricots
Juice of 1 lemon
Juice of 1 orange
1 teaspoon mild honey
1 large peach, peeled
¼ teaspoon dry mustard
¼ teaspoon cinnamon
½ cup plain low-fat yogurt

1. Place apricots in a bowl and pour on boiling water to cover. Let sit 10 minutes and drain.
2. Blend all ingredients, including apricots, until smooth in a blender or food processor. Refrigerate until ready to use.

Plum Sauce

Makes about 1 quart

This sauce is wonderful on toast or pancakes, or as a syrup on desserts. It also makes a nice gift.

2 pounds very ripe, juicy red plums, pitted and sliced
½ cup water
5 tablespoons mild honey
Juice of ½ lemon

1. Combine plums and water in an enameled, stainless steel or *Pyrex* saucepan and simmer 3 minutes. Add honey and return to a simmer, stirring. Remove from heat and let stand overnight (12 to 24 hours), covered with a towel or lid.
2. Bring mixture to a boil again and boil gently, stirring now and then, until plums break up and mixture thickens. Simmer about 1 hour and remove from heat. Add lemon juice and ladle into hot, sterilized jars.
3. Process in a boiling water bath 10 minutes, following directions in a canning guide.

Apricot Jam

1 pound pitted, dried apricots
3 tablespoons mild or medium honey
1 quart water
Juice and grated peel of 2 oranges
½ teaspoon almond extract

1. Combine apricots and water and let stand overnight, or for 8 to 12 hours.
2. Place mixture in a food processor or blender and blend in batches to a coarse purée. Transfer to a saucepan and add orange juice and rind and honey. Bring to a simmer and cook, stirring often, 20 to 30 minutes. Add almond extract and remove from heat.
3. Place jam in hot, sterilized jars and process in a boiling water bath 20 minutes, following the directions in a canning guide. Or, if eating right away, refrigerate in a covered container.

Mixed Fruit Chutney

Makes 2 quarts

1 cup cider vinegar
⅔ cup mild or medium honey
1 clove garlic, minced or pressed
1½ teaspoons freshly grated ginger, or ¾ teaspoon ground dried
¼ teaspoon freshly ground pepper
½ teaspoon ground cinnamon
1 tablespoon mustard seeds
½ teaspoon ground cloves
½ teaspoon ground coriander
½ teaspoon sea salt (optional)
2 medium tomatoes, peeled and diced
½ onion, chopped fine
2 apples, peeled and diced
2 pears, peeled and diced
½ cup raisins
½ cup chopped, dried figs

1. Combine all the ingredients in a large enameled or stainless steel saucepan and bring to a boil. Reduce heat, cover, and simmer 2 hours, until you have a chutney with a thick consistency.
2. Transfer to hot, sterilized jars and process in a boiling water bath 20 minutes. Cool and store in a cool, dry place. Once opened, keep refrigerated.

Opposite: Provencal Pizza (page 118).

Tomato Chutney

Makes 1 quart

1 pound apples, peeled, cored, and chopped
2 pounds fresh ripe tomatoes, chopped
2 ounces fresh ginger, finely minced or grated
1 cup cider vinegar
6 tablespoons mild or medium honey
1 small onion, minced
2 tablespoons raisins
1 teaspoon ground cardamom
½ teaspoon ground cloves
Sea salt to taste

Combine all the ingredients in a stainless steel or enameled saucepan and simmer 1 hour, uncovered. Ladle into hot, sterilized jars, wipe rims, and seal with canning lids. Process in boiling water 15 minutes. Cool. Refrigerate once opened. Store unopened jars in a cool, dark place.

Honey-Lemon Salad Dressing

2 tablespoons lemon juice
1 tablespoon mild honey
1 teaspoon Dijon mustard
Freshly ground black pepper
6 tablespoons safflower or vegetable oil

Stir together lemon juice, honey, mustard, and pepper. Whisk in oil. Toss with salad just before serving.

CHAPTER VIII

DESSERTS

Pear Almond Tart
Serves 8

For the crust:
¾ cup whole wheat pastry flour
¾ cup unbleached white flour
Pinch of sea salt
½ cup ground almonds
4 ounces unsalted butter
¼ teaspoon vanilla
½ teaspoon almond extract
1½ tablespoons mild honey

For the glaze:
1½ cups red wine
2 tablespoons lemon juice
2 tablespoons mild honey
1 stick cinnamon
1 teaspoon vanilla
1½ pounds ripe pears, peeled, cored, and quartered

DESSERTS

1 tablespoon cornstarch dissolved in 1 tablespoon water
For the rest of the tart:
½ lemon
1½ pounds firm ripe pears, cored, peeled, quartered
¼ cup blanched almonds

1. First make crust. Mix together flours, salt, and ground almonds and cut in butter. Add vanilla and almond extract and honey. The dough should come together like a normal, yet sticky, pie dough. If it is very crumbly add a teaspoon or more of ice cold water. Wrap and chill one to two hours.
2. Preheat oven to 375°F. Roll out pie crust and line a well-buttered 10 inch tart pan or pie dish with dough. The dough may be very crumbly when you roll it out. It might help to roll it out between pieces of waxed paper. Just persevere and patch it together if it falls apart.
3. Line tart shell with a sheet of aluminum foil and weight with ½ lb of dried beans. Bake 6 minutes in preheated oven. Remove lining and prick pastry shell in several places. Bake another 8 to 10 minutes, or until lightly browned. Cool on a rack.
4. Combine red wine, lemon juice, honey, cinnamon, and vanilla in a 2 quart saucepan and bring to a simmer. Simmer 5 minutes and drop in pears intended for glaze. Simmer 20 to 30 minutes. Remove cinnamon stick and purée pears through a food mill or in a blender. Return to poaching liquid and continue to cook over medium high heat until mixture is cooked down to 1½ cups. Dissolve cornstarch in a little water and add to purée, stirring. Turn down heat and simmer until mixture becomes a nice glaze, which should take only a minute or two.
5. Fill a bowl with water acidulated with the juice of ½ lemon. Peel and core remaining pears, cut into quarters, and drop into water. Drain carefully.
6. Pour all but ½ cup of the pear-wine purée into pie crust and spread evenly. Place pears over purée like petals of a flower. If they will not lie flat slice a flat edge along the bottom. With a very sharp, stainless steel knife cut thin slices across each quarter. Place 3 blanched almonds in each space between the petals, and the remaining almonds in the center. Spread remaining glaze evenly over the pears with a pastry brush. Serve.

Illustrated opposite page 176.

Almond-Granola Pie Crust

½ cup ground almonds

½ cup either rolled oats, granola, or muesli

1 cup whole wheat pastry flour

1 teaspoon ground cinnamon

¼ teaspoon sea salt

4 ounces unsalted butter

1-1½ tablespoons mild honey

1. Mix together ground almonds, oats, granola or muesli, whole wheat flour, cinnamon, and salt. Cut in butter. Add honey and gather into a ball.
2. Butter a tart pan and rather than rolling out the crust, press into pan. Fill pan by pressing portions of the dough from the center of the pan out flat with your fingers. Cover entire pan and pinch an attractive edge round the rim.
3. Refrigerate 1 to 2 hours and prebake 5 minutes at 350°F before filling.

Blueberry Tart

Serves 8

1 tart crust of your choice (pages 162 and 164)
1½ pounds blueberries
Juice of ½ lemon
3 tablespoons mild honey
1 tablespoon cornstarch
3 tablespoons Creme de Cassis liqueur

1. Preheat oven to 350°F. Prebake pie crust 5 minutes. Remove from heat and turn oven up to 450°F.
2. Toss together berries, lemon juice, and honey. Dissolve cornstarch in the Creme de Cassis and toss with berries. Turn into pie crust.
3. Place tart in oven and bake at high heat 10 minutes, then turn heat down to 350°F, and bake another 20 to 30 minutes, or until crust is nicely browned. Remove from heat and cool on a rack.

Pears Poached in Beaujolais with Peppercorns

Serves 6

6 comice pears

1 bottle Beaujolais

½ cup mild honey

2 tablespoons whole black peppercorns

1. Peel pears, leaving stems intact.
2. Combine Beaujolais, honey, and peppercorns in a saucepan and bring to a boil. Drop in pears, reduce heat, and simmer 15 minutes, or until the outside of pears is translucent but pears are still firm. Remove from the heat and allow to cool, then chill several hours. Should be served very cold.

Illustrated opposite page 176.

Pear Clafouti

Serves 6

1 tablespoon mild honey
Juice of ½ lemon
4 tablespoons either sweet white wine, eau de vie de poires, or Kirsch
1½ pounds firm, ripe pears, peeled, cored, and sliced

For the batter:

1 cup milk
2 tablespoons mild honey
3 eggs
1 tablespoon vanilla
Pinch of sea salt
6 level tablespoons unbleached white flour
6 level tablespoons whole wheat pastry flour
6 tablespoons liquid from the pears
Yogurt or cream for topping

1. Combine honey, lemon juice, and liquor. Place pears in a bowl and cover with alcohol mixture. Let sit 1 hour, tossing from time to time to marinate evenly.
2. Place milk, honey, eggs, vanilla, and salt in a blender and turn it on. Add flours while blender is running. Blend for 1 minute. If mixing by hand, blend together eggs and flour with a wooden spoon and whisk or beat in liquids. Strain through a fine strainer. Let batter rest 30 minutes.
3. Preheat oven to 350°F. Drain pears and add 6 tablespoons of their marinating liquid to batter. Butter a 2 quart flameproof baking dish and pour in a ¼ inch layer of batter. Place over a moderate flame 1 to 2 minutes, or until a film has set on the bottom. Now spread pears in a layer and pour on remaining batter.
4. Place in preheated oven and bake 45 minutes, or until puffed and brown and a knife plunged into the center comes out clean. Serve hot or warm, with a little cream or yogurt to moisten if you wish.

Honey-Poached Pears

Serves 4

2 cups dry white wine, preferably a Chablis or Chardonnay
½ cup mild honey
1 teaspoon vanilla extract, or ½ vanilla bean, split
2 tablespoons lemon juice
4 firm ripe pears
1 tablespoon chopped, fresh mint

1. Combine white wine, honey, vanilla, and lemon juice in a non-aluminum saucepan and bring to a boil. Reduce heat and maintain at a simmer.
2. Peel, quarter, and core pears and drop immediately into simmering wine. Simmer 15 minutes. Drain and pour liquid back into saucepan.
3. Boil down wine for about 10 minutes, or until you have about a cup and it is thick and amber colored.
4. Place pears in a serving bowl and pour in wine. Serve warm or chilled, garnished with mint. These can be refrigerated overnight.

Pumpkin Pie

1 dessert piecrust (page 164)
3 eggs
1 pound cooked, puréed pumpkin
1 cup milk
2 tablespoons butter
½ cup strong honey
1 tablespoon molasses
1½ teaspoons vanilla extract
2 teaspoons ground cinnamon
½ teaspoon ground ginger, or 1 teaspoon fresh, grated
¼ teaspoon mace
¼ teaspoon ground cloves
¼ teaspoon freshly grated nutmeg
1 tablespoon rum
¼ teaspoon sea salt
Whipped cream or plain yogurt

1. Preheat oven to 350°F. Roll out pie crust and line a 10 inch pie pan or tart pan. Beat 1 of the eggs and brush pie crust, then prebake 7 minutes. Remove from oven and turn up heat to 425°F.
2. Blend remaining eggs with rest of ingredients except whipped cream or yogurt. Pour into pie shell. Bake 10 minutes, then reduce heat to 350°F, and bake another 30 to 40 minutes, or until firm to the touch.
3. Cool and serve with whipped cream or plain yogurt.

Pumpkin Cake

3 cups sifted whole wheat pastry flour
2 teaspoons baking soda
2 teaspoons baking powder
1 tablespoon cinnamon
½ teaspoon powdered ginger
¼ teaspoon powdered cloves
¼ teaspoon nutmeg
¼ teaspoon allspice
¾ teaspoon sea salt
1 cup raisins
1 cup broken walnuts (optional)
1 cup mild, medium, or strong honey
1 cup safflower oil
2 cups cooked, puréed pumpkin
5 eggs
3 tablespoons rum
Butter for the pan
Whipped cream

1. Have all ingredients at room temperature. Preheat oven to 350°F and place rack in the lower half. Butter a bundt pan or a 10 × 4½ inch tube pan. If using a tube pan line with buttered waxed paper.
2. Sift together flour, baking soda, baking powder, spices, and sea salt. Add a tablespoon of the sifted dry ingredients to raisins in a small bowl, and toss with optional nuts to coat. Set aside.
3. Beat together honey and oil until creamy. Beat in pumpkin purée, then eggs, one at a time. Add rum. At low speed beat in dry ingredients, a cup at a time, scraping the sides of the bowl well. Beat only until smooth. Stir in raisins and nuts.
4. Turn into prepared pan and bake 1 hour and 5 minutes, or until a cake tester comes out dry. Cool on a rack for 10 minutes or so. Cake will only fill the pan ¾ full. Invert onto a rack, remove pan, and cool. Serve with whipped cream flavored with vanilla and rum.

Lemon Walnut Wafers
Makes 36

These are delicate, sweet, and tart. They are somewhat brittle.

¼ cup sifted soy flour
1¼ cups sifted whole wheat pastry flour
½ teaspoon baking powder
¼ teaspoon sea salt
⅛ teaspoon ground ginger
4 ounces butter
1 cup mild honey
1 egg plus 2 egg yolks
3-4 tablespoons lemon juice, to taste
Finely grated rind of 1 large lemon
½ teaspoon vanilla extract
½ cup walnuts, broken into medium pieces

1. Preheat oven to 350°F and adjust 2 oven racks to divide oven into thirds. Butter baking sheets.
2. Sift together flours, baking powder, salt, and ginger and set aside. Cream butter with honey. Add egg and egg yolks and beat until mixture is light and fluffy.
3. On low speed gradually add dry ingredients, scraping bowl and beating only until mixture is smooth. Beat in vanilla, lemon juice and rind, and stir in nuts.
4. Drop by rounded teaspoons onto biscuit sheets, 2 to 3 inches apart, as they spread. Bake 18 to 20 minutes, reversing sheets halfway through baking. The wafers do not brown on the tops, but they do around the edges. Cool on racks.

Apple Soufflé with Calvados

Serves 4 to 6

1 tablespoon butter
2 tablespoons wheat germ
1½ pounds cooking apples, peeled, cored, and halved
1⅓ cups water, acidulated with the juice of ½ lemon
6 tablespoons mild honey
½ teaspoon cinnamon
⅛ teaspoon freshly grated nutmeg
2 teaspoons cornstarch
1 additional tablespoon lemon juice
3 tablespoons Calvados
6 large egg whites, at room temperature
¼ teaspoon cream of tartar
Pinch of sea salt

1. Preheat oven to 425°F about 15 minutes before baking. Butter a 2 quart soufflé dish and dust with wheat germ. Refrigerate while you prepare soufflé mixture.
2. Slice half of 1 of the apples thinly. Place ½ cup of the acidulated water in a heavy saucepan, bring to a simmer, and poach apple slices 3 to 4 minutes. Drain and set aside.
3. Chop remaining apples fine and place in a medium saucepan with another ½ cup of the acidulated water and 1 tablespoon of honey. Bring to a simmer and cook uncovered 30 to 35 minutes, or until thick. Stir in cinnamon and nutmeg.
4. Combine remaining water and honey in a medium saucepan and bring to a boil. Boil 5 minutes and add to apple mixture. Bring to a simmer, stirring.
5. Dissolve cornstarch in remaining tablespoon of lemon juice and stir into apple mixture. Heat thoroughly, stirring, until nice and thick, about 5 minutes. Remove from heat, transfer to a mixing bowl, and stir in Calvados.
6. In another clean, dry mixing bowl beat egg whites until they begin to foam.

Add cream of tartar and a pinch of salt. Continue to beat until egg whites form stiff shiny peaks. Do not overbeat. Whisk ¼ of the egg whites into apple purée, combine thoroughly, and gently fold in rest.

7. Gently spoon soufflé mixture into prepared dish. It should come just about up to the top. Sprinkle poached apple slices over the surface and place immediately in preheated oven. Bake 16 to 17 minutes, or until well browned. Remove from oven, and serve at once.

Carob Sponge Roll

Even chocolate addicts (who always hate carob) have to admit that this is outstanding. It really does taste like chocolate. I think it's the combination of the coffee and carob chips.

Oil or butter for the baking pan
6 ounces carob chips or solid bar
2 teaspoons instant coffee, dissolved in 6 tablespoons hot water
8 large eggs, separated
Pinch of sea salt
½ cup mild honey
4-8 tablespoons carob powder, to taste
1 cup whipping cream
2 tablespoons mild honey
1 teaspoon vanilla
2 tablespoons Kahlua

1. Preheat oven to 350°F. Oil or butter a jelly roll pan and line it with waxed paper, with a 2 inch overhang on each end to serve as handles.
2. Dissolve carob nuggets or bar (break into pieces) in coffee in a small pan over low heat.
3. Beat egg yolks with a pinch of salt and honey at high speed in an electric mixer until mixture is very thick and somewhat stiff. Beat in carob-coffee mixture.
4. In a separate bowl beat egg whites with a pinch of salt until they form soft peaks. Be careful not to beat them too stiff, or you'll have trouble folding them into carob mixture. Stir ¼ of the beaten egg whites into egg yolk-carob mixture, then gently fold in remaining egg whites, or gently fold lightened egg yolk mixture into the whites, depending on which bowl is bigger.
5. Pour this mixture into prepared jelly roll pan and gently spread it evenly all over the surface. Bake in preheated oven 20 minutes, or until firm to the touch.
6. Dampen a dish towel or a length of 4 paper towels folded in half. When you pull the sponge out of the oven cover it immediately with the damp towel, and place a dry towel or length of paper towels over this. Let

DESSERTS

dessert roll cool, covered thus, until baking sheet is cool enough to handle.

7. Loosen sides of roll with a knife. Sprinkle top with carob powder. Place two lengths of waxed paper over top of sponge, and holding ends firmly, quickly reverse sponge roll and remove baking sheet. Now carefully remove waxed paper.

8. Beat cream in a chilled bowl until fairly stiff and add additional honey, vanilla, and Kahlua. Beat a little more. When sponge is cool enough so that it won't melt whipped cream, place dollops of cream all around the edges and spread all over the surface in a thick even layer.

9. Using the ends of the waxed paper as handles, and placing a board or platter, whatever you will be serving the roll on, at one edge of the roll, carefully roll up sponge lengthwise like a jelly roll, up onto serving surface. Cover with plastic wrap or waxed paper, and refrigerate until serving time, or freeze and thaw 15 minutes before you wish to serve.

Note: When you roll the sponge, don't be alarmed if it tears a little. It won't fall apart.

Carob Rum Raisin Cookies
Makes 48

1 cup raisins
½ cup dark rum
4 ounces carob chips
1½ cups sifted whole wheat pastry flour
¼ cup sifted soy flour
1 teaspoon baking powder
½ teaspoon baking soda
¼ teaspoon sea salt
4 ounces butter
1½ ounces vegetable margarine
¾ cup mild honey
1 teaspoon vanilla extract
1 egg
½ cup plain yogurt

1. Several hours or the day before you wish to bake, place raisins and rum in a saucepan and bring to a gentle boil. Remove from heat, cover, and let sit several hours or overnight. Drain excess rum and save for another purpose.

2. Preheat oven to 375°F and adjust racks to divide oven into thirds. Butter baking sheets or cut foil to lay over the racks.

3. Melt carob chips in top part of a double boiler over boiling water. Sift together flours, baking powder, baking soda, and salt and set aside. Cream margarine and butter, add vanilla and honey, and beat together well. Add egg and beat again, then beat in melted carob chips and yogurt. Gradually add dry ingredients, beating at low speed and scraping sides of bowl with a rubber spatula, only until ingredients are incorporated. Stir in raisins.

4. Drop by heaping teaspoons onto sheets or foil, leaving 2 inches between each cookie. Bake 15 to 20 minutes in preheated oven, reversing sheets top to bottom and front to back halfway through to ensure even baking. The cookies are done when they spring back lightly when pressed with fingertips. Remove from oven and cool on racks.

Opposite: Pear and Almond Tarte (page 162) and Pears Poached in Beaujolais with Peppercorns (page 166).

Oatmeal Carob Chip Cookies with Raisins and Nuts

1½ cups sifted whole wheat pastry flour
½ teaspoon sea salt
½ teaspoon baking soda
1 teaspoon cinnamon
½ teaspoon powdered cloves
½ teaspoon nutmeg
½ teaspoon allspice
1 cup wheat germ
½ pound vegetable margarine
1 cup mild honey
1 teaspoon vanilla extract
2 eggs
2 cups rolled oats
½ cup pitted dates, coarsely chopped
1 cup dark or golden raisins or currants
1 cup broken walnuts
1 cup carob chips

1. Preheat oven to 350°F.
2. Sift together flour, salt, baking soda, and spices and stir in wheat germ. Set aside.
3. Cream margarine and add honey. Beat well. Beat in vanilla and eggs. Slowly beat in oats, then dates and raisins, beating just enough to mix. Beat in sifted dry ingredients, a cup at a time, scraping bowl and beating only until mixed. Stir in nuts and carob chips.
4. Drop by large teaspoons onto foil-lined or buttered baking sheets, about 2 inches apart. Bake 12 to 14 minutes, reversing sheets halfway through baking, until cookies are golden brown and tops spring back if lightly pressed with a fingertip. Cool on racks.

Oatmeal Icebox Cookies

Makes 80 cookies

1 cup raisins or sultanas
Boiling water to cover the raisins
1 cup sifted whole wheat pastry flour
¼ cup sifted soy flour
1 teaspoon baking soda
½ teaspoon sea salt
¼ teaspoon ginger
1 teaspoon cinnamon
¼ teaspoon ground cloves
½ teaspoon nutmeg
½ cup wheat germ
½ pound vegetable margarine (can use half butter)
1¼ cups mild honey
1 teaspoon vanilla extract
2 teaspoons instant coffee
2 eggs
2½ cups rolled oats
1 cup chopped walnuts

1. Place raisins in a bowl and pour on boiling water to cover. Let sit 10 minutes, drain, and pat dry between pieces of paper towel.
2. Sift together flours, baking soda, salt, and spices. Stir in wheat germ and set aside.
3. Cream margarine and add honey, vanilla, and instant coffee. Beat well. Add eggs, one at a time, beating after each addition. Gradually add dry ingredients and rolled oats. Stir in raisins and nuts.
4. Spread out 2 pieces of waxed paper, about 13 to 15 inches long. Spoon batter onto sheets to make lengthwise log shapes, about 10 inches long, 2 inches wide, and 2 inches thick. Fold ends of paper up over ends and wrap sides. Place on a baking sheet and freeze 1 to 2 hours, or refrigerate overnight.
5. Preheat oven to 350°F. Slice dough with a thin. sharp knife into rounds

about ¼ inch thick. Place on foil-lined or buttered baking sheets, about 2 inches apart (they will spread). Bake 12 to 14 minutes, reversing baking sheets halfway through to ensure even baking. Let stand on the baking sheets for a few minutes, until they can be easily removed, then cool on racks. Store in an airtight jar.

Date Bars

Makes 24 bars

For the filling:
1½ pounds pitted dates, chopped
2 cups water
2 tablespoons lemon juice
2 tablespoons dark rum
Finely grated rind of 1 lemon
Finely grated rind of 1 orange
For the crust:
½ pound melted vegetable margarine
½ cup mild honey
4 tablespoons raw or date sugar
1½ cups sifted whole wheat pastry flour
¼ cup sifted soy flour
½ teaspoon sea salt
1½ cups rolled oats
½ cup walnuts, chopped medium fine

1. First make the filling. Place all ingredients except lemon and orange rind in a 2 quart saucepan and bring to a simmer, stirring occasionally. Simmer until thickened, stirring often, about 10 minutes. Stir in lemon and orange rind and set aside to cool while you prepare crust.

2. Preheat oven to 350°F, and adjust a rack a third of the way up from the bottom of the oven. Take an 8 x 12 inch oblong pan and line it with foil. Butter foil and spread half of the crust mixture over the bottom. It's easiest to do this with your hands; or use a spatula. It will be sticky, and the layer will be thin. Spread date mixture over this, and spread remaining crust over the date mixture, again most easily accomplished with the fingers.

3. Bake 45 minutes in preheated oven. Cool in pan 45 minutes.

4. Cover pan with a rack or baking sheet and invert. Remove pan and aluminum foil. Cover this with a rack and very carefully invert again. Cool completely, then chill briefly in the freezer until firm enough to cut. Cut into squares or bars with a long, very sharp knife. The bars will crumble a little. Wrap each bar individually in plastic wrap.

Champagne Sorbet
Serves 4

¾ cup mild honey
⅔ cup water
Grated rind of 2 oranges
Grated rind of 1 lemon
1 quart freshly squeezed orange juice, strained
Fresh juice of 1-2 lemons, to taste, strained
1 bottle Champagne, not too dry
½ cup Grand Marnier
Strawberries and mint for garnish

1. In a heavy-bottomed saucepan dissolve honey in water and simmer with orange and lemon peel 20 minutes.
2. Strain and add to orange and lemon juice, along with champagne and Grand Marnier. Stir well and freeze in ice-trays or a sorbettier. If using ice-trays, blend with an electric mixer or food processor halfway through the freezing to break up the ice crystals.
3. Let soften in refrigerator 30 minutes before serving if frozen solid. Serve garnished with strawberries and fresh mint.

Pineapple Banana Mint Sherbet

Serves 4

½ cup orange juice
2 tablespoons fresh mint, plus additional for garnish
1 large, ripe pineapple, peeled, cored, and coarsely chopped
1 tablespoon fresh lime juice
2 tablespoons mild honey
1 large ripe banana

1. Blend orange juice and mint together in a blender until mint is very finely chopped, or liquified. Blend in remaining ingredients, except garnish, and purée until smooth.
2. Pour into ice trays or a baking dish and freeze until just beginning to set. Remove from freezer and beat with an electric mixer, a whisk, or in a food processor to break up ice crystals. Place in freezer again and repeat once more when just beginning to set.
3. Pack into a container and freeze. If frozen solid, let soften in refrigerator 1 hour before serving. Serve garnished with fresh mint.

Brown Rice Pudding

Serves 4 to 6

3 eggs
Pinch of sea salt
1½ cups milk
½ cup mild honey
1 teaspoon vanilla
2 teaspoons grated lemon peel
1 tablespoon lemon juice
½ teaspoon cinnamon
¼ teaspoon ground nutmeg
½ cup dark or golden raisins
2 apples, cored and chopped
2 cups cooked brown rice
Plain low-fat yogurt for topping

1. Preheat oven to 325°F.
2. Beat eggs together with sea salt, milk, and honey. Stir in vanilla, lemon peel, lemon juice, the spices, raisins, apples, and the rice.
3. Place in a buttered 1½ or 2 quart baking dish or soufflé dish and bake 50 minutes in preheated oven until set. Serve warm or cold, topped with yogurt.

Honey Cakes

Honey cakes are dense, with a close crumb and moist texture. These age well and can even be frozen. The spice cakes are best wrapped for a few days before cutting, so that the spicy aromas have time to ripen. The cakes should be sliced thin, for they are fairly heavy. They are good as a snack or as an accompaniment with fruit desserts. They can be served with a dollop of whipped cream.

Jewish Honey Cake

1¾ cups sifted whole wheat pastry flour
⅛ teaspoon sea salt
¾ teaspoon baking powder
½ teaspoon baking soda
¼ teaspoon ground ginger
⅛ teaspoon freshly grated nutmeg
⅛ teaspoon ground cloves
2 eggs
¼ cup safflower oil
1 cup medium or dark honey
¼ cup cold coffee
¾ cup chopped walnuts

1. Preheat oven to 325°F. Butter a 9 x 5 inch loaf pan.
2. Sift together all the dry ingredients.
3. Beat together eggs, oil, and honey. Beat until thick and lemon-colored. Add coffee, then flour mixture, a little at a time, beating slowly. Stir until batter is smooth.
4. Turn into prepared pan. Bake about 50 minutes or longer, until cake is browned and a cake tester comes out clean. Cool in pan 10 minutes, then carefully turn out onto a rack to cool. Wrap in plastic wrap and foil and store for a few days before cutting (if you have the will power). This one can also be eaten the day it is baked.

Dark Honey Cake

2 tablespoons halved almonds
1 cup sifted unbleached white flour
1½ cups sifted whole wheat pastry flour
1½ teaspoons cinnamon
½ teaspoon freshly grated nutmeg
½ teaspoon ground cardamom
¼ teaspoon ground ginger
¼ teaspoon ground cloves
2 teaspoons baking soda
Pinch of sea salt
4 ounces butter
1 cup dark honey
6 eggs, separated
Grated rind of 1 lemon
½ cup milk

1. Preheat oven to 375°F. Butter a 10 inch tube pan or a spring form pan and sprinkle almonds over the bottom.
2. Sift together flours, spices, baking soda, and sea salt.
3. Cream together butter and honey. Add egg yolks and lemon rind.
4. Add flour mixture in batches, alternating with milk and ending with flour, to butter mixture, beating between additions.
5. Beat egg whites until stiff but not dry, and carefully fold into batter. Pour batter into prepared cake pan and place in preheated oven. Bake 40 minutes. Reduce heat to 325°F and bake another 20 to 30 minutes, or until a cake tester comes out clean. Cool 10 minutes in the pan, then carefully turn out onto a rack and cool. Wrap well and store for a few days before cutting.

Whole Wheat Lemon Yogurt Cake

4 ounces butter
½ cup mild honey
3 eggs, separated
1 whole egg
½ teaspoon vanilla
Juice of ½ large lemon (about 2½ tablespoons)
Grated rind of 1 lemon
½ cup plain yogurt
1½ cups unbleached white flour
1½ cups whole wheat pastry flour
2 teaspoons baking powder
Pinch of sea salt

1. Preheat oven to 350°F. Butter a 9 × 5 inch loaf pan.
2. Cream together butter and honey. Beat in egg yolks and whole egg. Add vanilla, lemon juice, lemon rind, and yogurt.
3. Sift together flours, baking powder, and salt. Gradually mix dry ingredients into butter-honey mixture.
4. Beat egg whites until glossy and gently fold in. Carefully pour into baking pan. Bake 1 hour, or until browned and a cake tester comes out clean. Cool in pan, then remove and wrap well to store.

Note: This will keep 2 to 3 days. It has a very dense texture.

INDEX OF HERB RECIPES

Beans with Coriander, Black or Pinto, 85
Beet Salad, 123
  Middle Eastern, 126
Blender "Bearnaise", 151
Borscht, Turkish, 64
Brown Rice and Basil Eggah, 112
Brown Rice and Basil Gratin, 111

Cacik, 130
Caraway Coleslaw, 125
Carottes Rapées (Grated Carrot Salad), 131
Carrot Salad, Moroccan, 140
Carrots with Caraway Seeds, 84
Cheese, Bread, and Tomato Casserole, 121
Cheese Spread, Herbed, 110
Chickpea and Cumin Dip, 87
Chive Crêpes, 114
Chutney, Mixed Fruit, 160
Coriander-Cumin Tomato Sauce, 145
Coriander Sauce, 146
Coucou à l'Iranien, 117
Cucumber Salad with Feta Cheese Dressing, 139
Cucumbers, Fresh Dilled, 135

Dill and Cottage Cheese Casserole Bread, 46
Dill Soup, Hot or Chilled, 63

Eggs with Chives, Scrambled, 115

Eggs with Fines Herbes, Soft-Boiled, 109
Eggplant Purée, Spicy, 84
Eggplant Salad, Lebanese, 127

Fines Herbes Butter, 106

Goulash, Red Bean, 82

Herb Vinegars, 143

Kasha with Mushrooms and Dill, 88

Lentil and Sorrel Soup, 62
Lentil Salad, 133
Lentils and Bulghur with Parsley and Mint, 92
Lentils, Spicy, 95

Melon, Cucumber, and Tomato Salad, 132
Minted Breakfast Drink, 31
Mushroom and Fennel Salad with Lime Vinaigrette, 137
Mushrooms Caps, Broiled, 94
Mushrooms Stuffed with Pesto, 79
Mustard, Coarse-Ground, with Red Wine and Garlic, 156

Omelette Aux Fines Herbes, 108

Pain d'Épices, 50
Parsley Purée, 94

Pasta e Fagiole, 90
Pasta, Spiral, with Rich Tomato Sauce, 82
Pilaki (Turkish Cooked Vegetable Salad), 128
Pineapple, Banana Mint Sherbet, 182
Pizza, Provençal, 118
Potato Soup with Chervil, 67
Potatoes, New, with Dill, 88
Potatoes with Pesto, 78
Pumpernickel, Moist, 48
Pumpkin Soup, Curried, 71
   Puréed, 70

Quiche Aux Fines Herbes, 107

Red Cabbage and Apple Salad with Poppy Seed Dressing, 142
Rice with Tofu, Potatoes, and Cumin, 86
Romaine and Mushroom Salad with Fennel, 136
Rye and Sage Muffins, 54
Rye and Whole Wheat Bread, Herbed, 51
Rye Caraway Soup, 68
Rye-Oatmeal Bread with Anise and Raisins, 52

Salad, Middle Eastern, 134
Salad with Marjoram, Tossed, 138
Salade Mesclun (Mixed Greens Salad), 129
Salade Verte Aux Champignons, 130
Sandwich Loaf, Mediterranean, 116
Sorrel Omelette, 119
Sorrel Soup, 63

Soup, Black Bean, 65
Spinach and Bulghur Salad with Poppy Seed Dressing, 141
Spinach Gnocchi with Sage Butter, 120
Sweet and Sour Leeks, 97
   Red Peppers, 96

Tarragon Mustard, 157
Tarragon Soup, 72
Tofu and Broccoli with Fennel, 89
Tofu Remoulade Sauce, 150
Tomato and Mozzarella Salad with Pesto, 124
Tomato Ketchup, Homemade, 154
Tomato-Mint Sauce, 147
Tomato-Sage Sauce, 149
Tomato Sauce, Tofu, 148
   Very Quick, Very Fresh, 147
   with Basil, 144
Tomato Soup with Basil, Cold, 69
Tomatoes and Zucchini Stuffed with Lentils and Bulghur, 93

Vegetable Stock, 61

White Beans, Greek Style, 81

Yogurt Soup with Coriander, Hot, 66

Ziti with Tomato-Basil Sauce and Cheese, Baked, 113
Zucchini Gratin, 91
Zucchini with Yogurt and Mint, 139

INDEX OF HONEY RECIPES

Acorn Squash, Baked, 101
Almond-Granola Pie Crust, 164
Apple Soufflé with Calvados, 172
Apricot Jam, 159

Banana Nut Muffins, 57
Banana-Yogurt Breakfast Drink, 25
Beans with Fruit, Baked, 103
Blueberry Tart, 165
Brown Rice Pudding, 183
Buckwheat Pancakes, 38

Cabbage with Apples, Cooked, 100

Carob Rum Raisin Cookies, 176
Carob Sponge Roll, 174
Carrot Salad, Shredded, with Poppy Seed Dressing, 142
Challah, Holiday, 42
Champagne Sorbet, 181
Cherry-Lemon Soup, Cold, 74
Chutney, Mixed Fruit, 160
   Tomato, 161
Coffee Cake, Braided Fruit-Filled, 26
Cornbread, Texas, 47
Couscous with Honey and Fruit, 29
Cranberry Soup with Pomegranate Seeds, Chilled, 77

INDEX OF HONEY RECIPES

Date Bars, 180

Fig and Walnut Bread, 44
Fruit Curry, 102
Fruit Soup, 76

Granola, Fancy, 34

Honey Cake, Dark, 34
    Jewish, 184
Honey-Lemon Salad Dressing, 161
Honeyed Yogurt Cereal Topping, 36

Lemon Walnut Wafers, 171

Melon, Cucumber, and Tomato Salad, 132
Melon Soup, Chilled, 74
Muesli, Mixed Grains, 33
Muffins, Zucchini-Carrot, 56
    Leftover Grains, 59
    Wheat Germ and Fruit, 58

Oatmeal Carob Chip Cookies with Raisins and Nuts, 177
Oatmeal, Cornmeal, and Honey Bread, 40
Oatmeal Icebox Cookies, 178
Oatmeal with Fruit and Honey, 30
Onions Cooked in Red Wine, 99
Orange Date Muffins, 55
Orange Peach Dressing, 158

Pain Perdu (French Toast), 32

Peach-Yogurt Soup, 75
Peanut Butter Tofu Spread, 28
Pear Almond Tart, 162
Pear Clafouti, 167
Pears, Honey-Poached, 168
Pears Poached in Beaujolais with Peppercorns, 166
Pineapple Banana Mint Sherbet, 182
Plum Sauce, 158
Poppy Seed Dressing, 152
Potato Soufflé, Sweet, 122
Potato Soup, Sweet, 73
Pumpkin Cake, 170
Pumpkin Pie, 169
Pumpkin Stuffed with Millet and Fruit, 104
Purée of Sweet Potatoes with Apple, 98

Russian Dressing, Low-Fat, 152

Salad Dressing, Oriental, 153
Scones, 60
Semolina with Raisins and Cinnamon, 37
Strawberry Omelette, 36
Sweet and Sour Leeks, 97
    Red Peppers, 96

Tahini-Tamari Sauce, 155
Tofu Spread, Morning, 35
Tomato Ketchup, Homemade, 154

Whole Wheat Lemon Yogurt Cake, 186

Yogurt Pancakes, 39

GENERAL INDEX

Acorn Squash, Baked, 101
Almond-Granola Pie Crust, 164
anise, 10
Apple Soufflé with Calvados, 172
Apricot Jam, 159

Banana Nut Muffins, 57
banana-Yogurt Breakfast Drink, 25
basil, 10
bay leaves, 11
Beans with Coriander, Black or Pinto, 85
Beans with Fruit, Baked, 103
Beetroot Salad, 123
    Middle Eastern, 126
Blender "Bearnaise", 151
Blueberry Tart, 165
Borscht, Turkish, 64

bouquet garni, 11
Brown Rice and Basil Eggah, 112
Brown Rice and Basil Gratin, 111
Brown Rice Pudding, 183
Buckwheat Pancakes, 38

Cabbage with Apples, Cooked, 100
Cacik, 130
caraway, 11
Caraway Coleslaw, 125
Carob Rum Raisin Cookies, 176
Carob Sponge Roll, 174
Carottes Rapées (Grated Carrot Salad), 131
Carrot Salad, Moroccan, 140
Carrot Salad, Shredded, with Poppy Seed Dressing, 142

Carrots with Caraway Seeds, 84
cayenne, 12
Challah, Holiday, 42
Champagne Sorbet, 181
Cheese, Bread, and Tomato Casserole, 121
Cheese Spread, Herbed, 110
Cherry-Lemon Soup, Cold, 74
chervil, 12
Chickpea and Cumin Dip, 87
Chive Crêpes, 114
chives, 12
Chutney, Mixed Fruit, 160
  Tomato, 161
cilantro, see coriander
Coffee Cake, Braided Fruit-Filled, 26
coriander, 12
Coriander-Cumin Tomato Sauce, 145
Coriander Sauce, 146
Cornbread, Texas, 47
Coucou à l'Iranien, 117
Couscous with Honey and Fruit, 29
Cranberry Soup with Pomegranate Seeds, Chilled, 77
Cucumber Salad with Feta Cheese Dressing, 138
Cucumbers, Fresh Dilled, 135
cumin, 13

Date Bars, 180
David, Elizabeth, 8, 9
dill, 13
Dill and Cottage Cheese Casserole Bread, 46
Dill Soup, Hot or Chilled, 63

Eggs with Chives, Scrambled, 115
Eggs with Fines Herbes, Soft-Boiled, 109
Eggplant Purée, Spicy, 84
Eggplant Salad, Lebanese, 127

fennel, 13-14
Fig and Walnut Bread, 44
fines herbes, 14
Fines Herbes Butter, 106
Fruit Curry, 102
Fruit Soup, 76

Goulash, Red Bean, 82
Granola, Fancy, 34

herb gardens, 7, 9
Herb Vinegars, 143
herbs, drying, 9-10
  freezing, 10
  storing fresh, 9
  types of, 10-17

honey, consistency of, 23-24
  cooking with, 20
  nutritional information, 19
  production of, by bees, 17-19
  storing, 20
  types of, mild, 21-22
    medium, 22
    strong, 22-23
  virtues of, over sugar, 19
Honey Cake, Dark, 185
  Jewish, 184
Honey-Lemon Salad Dressing, 161
Honeyed Yogurt Cereal Topping, 36

Kasha with Mushrooms and Dill, 88

Lemon Walnut Wafers, 171
Lentil and Sorrel Soup, 62
Lentil Salad, 133
Lentils and Bulghur with Parsley and Mint, 92
Lentils, Spicy, 95

marjoram, 14
Melon, Cucumber, and Tomato Salad, 132
Melon Soup, Chilled, 74
mint, 14
Minted Breakfast Drink, 31
Muesli, Mixed Grains, 33
Muffins, Zucchini-Carrot, 56
  Leftover Grains, 59
  Wheat Germ and Fruit, 58
Mushroom and Fennel Salad with Lime Vinaigrette, 137
Mushroom Caps, Broiled, 94
Mushrooms Stuffed with Pesto, 79
Mustard, Coarse-Ground, with Red Wine and Garlic, 156

Oatmeal Carob Chip Cookies with Raisins and Nuts, 177
Oatmeal, Cornmeal, and Honey Bread, 40
Oatmeal Icebox Cookies, 178
Oatmeal with Fruit and Honey, 30
Omelette Aux Fines Herbes, 108
Onions Cooked in Red Wine, 99
Orange Date Muffins, 55
Orange Peach Dressing, 158
oregano, 14

Pain d'Épices, 50
Pain Perdu (French Toast), 32
parsley, 15
Parsley Purée, 94
Pasta e Fagiole, 90
Pasta, Spiral, with Rich Tomato Sauce, 82

GENERAL INDEX

Peach-Yogurt Soup, 75
Peanut Butter Tofu Spread, 28
Pear Almond Tart, 162
Pears, Honey-Poached, 168
Pears, Poached in Beaujolais with Peppercorns, 166
Pilaki (Turkish Cooked Vegetable Salad), 128
Pineapple Banana Mint Sherbet, 182
Pizza, Provençal, 118
Plum Sauce, 158
Poppy Seed Dressing, 152
Potato Soufflé, Sweet, 122
Potato Soup, Sweet, 73
Potato Soup with Chervil, 67
Potatoes, New, with Dill, 88
Potatoes with Pesto, 78
Pumpernickel, Moist, 48
Pumpkin Cake, 170
Pumpkin Pie, 169
Pumpkin Soup, Curried, 71
Puréed, 70
Pumpkin Stuffed with Millet and Fruit, 104
Purée of Sweet Potatoes with Apple, 98

Quiche Aux Fines Herbes, 107

Red Cabbage and Apple Salad with Poppy Seed Dressing, 142
Rice with Tofu, Potatoes, and Cumin, 86
Romaine and Mushroom Salad with Fennel, 136
rosemary, 15
Russian Dressing, Low-Fat, 152
Rye and Sage Muffins, 54
Rye and Whole Wheat Bread, Herbed, 51
Rye Caraway Soup, 68
Rye-Oatmeal Bread with Anise and Raisins, 52

sage, 15-16
Salad Dressing, Oriental, 153
Salad, Middle Eastern, 134
Salad with Marjoram, Tossed, 139
Salade Mesclun (Mixed Greens Salad), 129
Salade Verte Aux Champignons, 130
Sandwich Loaf, Mediterranean, 116

savory, summer, 16
Scones, 60
Semolina with Raisins and Cinnamon, 37
sorrel, 16
Sorrel Omelette, 119
Sorrel Soup, 63
Soup, Black Bean, 65
Spinach and Bulghur Salad with Poppy Seed Dressing, 141
Spinach Gnocchi with Sage Butter, 120
Strawberry Omelette, 36
Summer Cooking, 8
Sweet and Sour Leeks, 97
Red Peppers, 96

Tahini-Tamari Sauce, 155
tarragon, 16-17
Tarragon Mustard, 157
Tarragon Soup, 72
thyme, 17
Tofu and Broccoli with Fennel, 89
Tofu Remoulade Sauce, 150
Tofu Spread, Morning, 35
Tomato and Mozzarella Salad with Pesto, 124
Tomato Ketchup, Homemade, 154
Tomato-Mint Sauce, 147
Tomato-Sage Sauce, 149
Tomato Sauce, Tofu, 148
Very Quick, Very Fresh, 147
with Basil, 144
Tomato Soup with Basil, Cold, 69
Tomato and Zucchini Stuffed with Lentils and Bulghur, 93

Vegetable Stock, 61

White Beans, Greek Style, 83
Whole Wheat Lemon Yogurt Cake, 186

Yogurt Pancakes, 39
Yogurt Soup with Coriander, Hot, 66

Ziti with Tomato-Basil Sauce and Cheese, Baked, 113
Zucchini Gratin, 91
Zucchini with Yogurt and Mint, 138